Catherine Grady Crabtree's

À LA
NEW ORLEANS

RESTAURANT RECIPES

by
MICHAEL GRADY

PUBLISHER:
CATHERINE GRADY CRABTREE

ASSISTANT TO THE PUBLISHER:
BEVERLY DONOHUE

ILLUSTRATIONS:
PAMELA DUNGAN

RECIPES TESTED BY:
J & L CATERING

COVER ART:
JIM HENDERSON

CRABTREE PUBLISHING

Printed in the United States of America
Published by Crabtree Publishing
P.O. Box 3451
Federal Way, Washington 98003

For additional copies write directly
to Crabtree Publishing
or use order forms in back of book.

I.S.B.N. 0-937070-02-5

II

Notes From Test Kitchen
by
Jane Egger
and
Linda Schmidt

New Orleans is a city of many different traditions such as Southern, French, Creole and Spanish. *A La New Orleans* captures the spirit of those traditions. The chefs of the city have presented recipes that are divergent in mood and taste, but all delicious.

We have tested the recipes and where necessary, simplified them so that they are easy to prepare in your own kitchens. In some cases, the recipes call for special regional ingredients. When appropriate we have recommended substitutes readily available in supermarkets or gourmet shops.

In the book are recipes for the most traditional Southern dinner or the most elegant continental cuisine. We urge you to try them all for a delicious taste of New Orleans!

TABLE OF CONTENTS

Acknowledgement

I had visited New Orleans once before. Spring vacation was a burned-out body returning north to school. It was a brief, nocturnal visit. The hours were spent swilling beer and leaning for the cue ball in rancid, dimly-lit rooms.

Nine years later I returned to New Orleans to investigate that city's famous restaurants. My credentials were a grasp of the fork, knife and spoon and a familiarization with the Mississippi. The first appointment was at "Masson's". I was forty-five minutes late and without questions, punctuated by my failure to ask the proprietor, a sommelier, if I might see the cellar. Things did improve. The next five weeks unraveled the mysteries of bearnaise, bouillabaise and hollandaise; my confidences grew.

The following pages reflect the hospitality and patience of the restaurant owners, their representatives, the chefs, the Louisiana Tourist Commission, the innkeepers and finally, the many pedestrians and gas station attendants who served as my compass and always knew True North.

M. G.

Introduction

Although my investigations centered on restaurants whose compliments far outweigh criticism, let it be known my Midwestern practicality drove me in quest of good food not just haute cuisine. When led by reports of memorable meals, I approached paper napkins as eagerly as creased linen. My notebook's pages evidence this flexibility-within worn borders reside remnants of ketchup, collard greens and cornbread as well as Marchand DeVin, crepes and white asparagus.

While restaurants were the focus of my attentions, lack of dietary discipline plus an active curiosity directed me to a neighborhood bakery, a French pastry shop, ice cream parlors, early A.M. cafes, a grocery store that clings to early twentieth century traditions and dispensers of the city's wines. My impressions of these additional visits will be found in either the body of this book or the final overview. Further ventures will go unreported to avoid stirring doubts of my singleness of purpose. However, if the readership expresses interest in an occasional non-caloric view of a city, future efforts could make such accommodations.

Like other metropolitan areas, New Orleans' cultural diversity is found in her kitchens. Unlike other large cities, New Orleans' cuisine moves beyond pure ethnic and is dominated by Creole cooking and its country cousin-Cajun cooking. Each has its own unique origin, but both opened their pots early to Latin, Negro, Indian and Spanish influences. Creole cuisine had its beginnings with the arrival of the French in Louisiana around 1690. It is characterized as the food of the city-sophisticated recipes, combining subtle seasonings and secret sauces, served in elegant settings to the powdered and perfumed. Cajun cuisine arrived with the Acadians in the 1750's. It is thought of as the food of the bayou-basic, biting, sustaining, served in simple settings to those whose hands boast callouses not manicures.

— Continued —

Whether the focus of your attentions is Creole or Cajun, Louisiana's kitchens are scenes of improvisation. There is little cooking by the book. There is no one recipe for the perfect gumbo, jambalaya, grillade or roux. This tendency to experiment may be due to the heterogeneous nature of these two cuisines and the inclination of cooks to continue this tradition. The high degree of success such experimentation brings may be partially due to most Louisianan's early introduction to that state's natural storehouse of foods. Within easy access are tidewaters, lakes, rivers, marshlands, piney woods and fields, yielding everything from strawberries to oysters. Youngsters watch crabs langour in traps and tumult in pots, wipe creole tomatoes clean on faded denim and confess early addiction to oyster liquor. In short, they have a running start in the kitchen.

The result of the intermingling of these foods under varied techniques appear in the following pages. There are appetizers, entrees, side dishes, desserts and cordials. You will find broth, bisque, Gazpacho, gumbo, bouillebaisse and minestrone. There are recipes for breakfast, lunch and dinner. A variety of preparations utilize beef, poultry, pork, veal, fish and shellfish. You will learn with what to stuff mushrooms, eggplants, avocadoes and bell peppers. The desserts are with dough and without, flamed and iced, including cakes, crepes, custard, parfaits, pies, puddings and souffles.

If the test kitchen has succeeded in its attempts to insure the successful recreation of these recipes in your homes, you should experience many times over the fabulous creations that have long occupied my mind, but too seldom my table.

The Andrew Jackson

Patrons of the Andrew Jackson are knowledgeable people. They know the rewards that wait just beyond the white, double doors on Royal Street. If their tastes lean to veal they know that King Ferdinands I through VI had nothing over the VII, unless one finds fault with veal slices sauteed in butter and asparagus then covered with crabmeat and topped with bearnaise sauce. They know of a treasure Jean Lafitte missed, yet which bears his name. *Crabmeat Lafitte* boasts ample amounts of lump crabmeat sauteed in subtle seasonings, dry wine and covered with a buttery hollandaise. Those who order the sherried turtle soup suddenly know a great version from those that are too often only fair. Regular customers know that The Andrew Jackson has one of New Orleans' hottest shrimp remoulades, popular flaming desserts and homemade ice cream.

— Continued —

The Andrew Jackson's decor and atmosphere have a habit of quelling the restive spirit. A plummeting Dow Jones and parental woes are left in the cloakroom. The luncheon hour is a time of marked levity. Festive conversation permeates a dining room embellished with a four hundred year old Austrian Father Time Clock, a rare, lavender marble mantle and imported, crystal chandeliers. Dinners are a softly lit, but no less light affair. Warm glows from tabled candles are recaptured on a mirrored ceiling, gold-leafed wallpaper and the crystal chandeliers.

It usually takes no longer than the arrival of the appetizer to appreciate the dining room staff. They must rank as one of New Orleans' most efficient, enthusiastic and attractive.

The Andrew Jackson, with competitively priced French and Creole cuisine serves lunch and dinner.

Crab Meat Lafitte

A LA - The Andrew Jackson

— Hollandaise Sauce —

4	egg yolks	¼	cup water
2	T. tarragon vinegar	⅛	t. salt
¼	lb. butter (melted)	3	dashes of Tabasco

— Crab Meat Lafitte —

¼	lb. oleo or butter		salt & pepper (to taste)
2	green onions	2	oz. sherry wine
¼	medium white onion	4	halves of toast
1	lb. lump crabmeat	1	dash of paprika

— Hollandaise Sauce —

1. Add vinegar to yolks and beat until light in color.
2. Place yolks in top of double boiler and cook slightly. Add butter slowly (drop by drop) beating all the while with beater until sauce becomes thick. (If it becomes too thick, you may add a little water).
3. Add salt and three dashes of Tabasco; blend and keep hot.

— Crab Meat Lafitte —

4. Melt butter in a large saucepan over medium heat and saute green and white onions until limp. Add crabmeat, salt and pepper and blend. Add sherry wine and simmer.
5. Slice each half of toast in half again. Place two pieces on each plate. Spoon crab mixture on top and overlay with hollandaise.

Serves: 4
Preparation: 35 minutes

Chicken Rochambeau

═══════════════════════════════

A LA - The Andrew Jackson

4 chicken breasts (boned)
  salt
  flour
½ lb. margarine
3 cups beef base or beef stock (not bouillon)
½ cup dry white wine

— Marchand de Vin Sauce —

1 green onion (sliced)
¼ lb. fresh mushrooms (sliced)
¼ lb. butter
1½ cups beef base (leftover from chicken)
¼ cup dry red wine
  salt
2 T. flour

2 slices of toast (halved)
4 slices ham or Canadian bacon (broiled)
1 cup Bearnaise Sauce (use canned or packaged variety)
  paprika

1. Salt breasts. Dust with flour and saute them in margarine. Cook about ten minutes.
2. Heat beef base; add white wine and breasts. Simmer for ten minutes. Remove, keep warm.

— Marchand de Vin Sauce —

3. Saute onion and mushrooms in butter; add beef base and red wine. Salt to taste, and add flour to thicken. Stir until smooth.

— Continued —

4

4. Place one half toast slice in center of dinner plate. Arrange broiled ham or Canadian bacon on top of toast. Top with Marchand de Vin Sauce. Place breast on top and overlay with Bearnaise; sprinkle with paprika.

Serves: 4
Preparation: 10 minutes
Cooking: 50 minutes

Delicious combination — very filling!

Lobster Savannah

A LA - The Andrew Jackson

2	whole lobsters *
½	cup butter
½	green pepper (diced)
½	small white onion (diced)
¼	lb. mushrooms (sliced)
¼	cup + 1 T. flour
2	cups milk (heated)
1	T. pimento
	salt (to taste)
	pepper (to taste)
2½	ounces sherry
	cheddar cheese (grated)

1. In a pot with boiling water, boil lobsters for five minutes. Reduce heat and simmer for fifteen minutes. When cooked, cut lobsters in half and remove meat. Save shells and set meat aside.
2. In a skillet with melted butter, saute pepper and onion until onion is transparent. Add mushrooms. Slowly add flour and blend til smooth.
3. Heat milk separately and slowly add to mixture, stirring to make a smooth consistency. Add pimento, salt, pepper and continue to simmer the sauce while adding sherry.
4. Preheat oven to 425°. Add lobster meat to sauce. Stir and heat thoroughly.
5. Stuff shells with lobster mixture. Top with cheese and put in oven to brown.

Serves: 4
Preparation: 35 minutes
Baking: 10 minutes

---

* If you prefer, you may substitute frozen tails as we did in our test kitchen. Since the dish is rich and filling, one small-medium tail per person is adequate.

Oysters Bienville

A LA - The Andrew Jackson

¼	cup butter or margarine
1	T. shrimp (chopped)
1	medium onion (chopped)
¼	lb. mushrooms (chopped)
¼	cup flour
¼	cup milk
¼	cup sherry
¼	cup catsup
	dash thyme
	bay leaf
2	dozen medium oysters

1. Melt butter in large pan; add shrimp, onion and mushrooms and saute until onion is limp. Add flour stirring until smooth. Gradually stir in milk, sherry, catsup, thyme and bay leaf. Cook sauce over low heat for five minutes. Preheat oven to 350°.
2. Meanwhile bring four cups water to boil; add oysters and cook for five - ten minutes.
3. Remove oysters to buttered ovenproof pan; cover with sauce.
4. Bake in oven for 15 - 20 minutes. Serve immediately.

Serves: 4
Preparation: 20 minutes
Baking: 15 - 20 minutes

ANTOINE'S

Founded by Antoine Alciatore in 1840, Antoine's may be the oldest restaurant in America and certainly one of the most famous. It is often the reference point from which competition is measured with regards to tradition, style and cuisine.

To visit Antoine's is to step into the past. Such notables as Florenz Ziegfeld, Cecil B. DeMille, Sarah Bernhardt and Franklin D. Roosevelt have dined here. The main dining room retains its original decor, consisting of a white-tiled floor, Victorian brass chandeliers and translucent pleated drapes. During daylight hours this room is swathed in light worthy of a diefic diner. One of several private dining areas is the 1840 Room. Modeled after a small dining room of the same period, its walls are laden with Alciatore mementoes and other memorabilia.

— Continued —

Quality food and innovative recipes are what made Antoine's a success. Many popular appetizers include *Oysters Rockefeller*, an Antoine's creation whose rich sauce gives meaning to its namesake. Entrees like *Boeuf Robespierre*, *Pompano en Papillote* and *Chicken Rochambeau* captivate diners raised on spoons of even the purest silver. Spud lovers should make the *Souffle Potatoes* a gastronomical obligation. A formidable list of desserts include *Peach Melba*, *Chocolate Mousse*, *Crepes Suzettes* and *Baked Alaska*.

Because Antoine's menu is in French, patrons often rely on the suggestions of their waiters. This talented staff also provides diners with a degree of entertainment by putting orders to memory rather than to paper.

Jackets and reservations are required.

A LA - Antoine's _

2 lbs. California potatoes (or 1 potato per person)
1 deep fat fryer with oil at moderate temperature
1 deep fat fryer with oil at very hot temperature
salt (to taste)

1. Peel potatoes and cut into long narrow slices, one eighth inch thick.
2. Put slices in wire basket and wash with cold water to remove excess starch. Dry.
3. Place a few potato slices at a time in moderate hot fat. When edges begin to puff slightly transfer to very hot fat.
4. Cook until fully puffed and golden brown.
5. Drain on absorbant paper. Sprinkle with salt and serve at once.

Preparation: 15 minutes
Cooking: 15 - 20 minutes
Serves: 6

Eggs Sardou

A LA - Antoine's

— Hollandaise Sauce —

1	cup butter	3	peppercorns
2	T. tarragon vinegar	4	egg yolks
1	T. water		juice of ¼ lemon
1	T. onion (minced)		

8   artichoke hearts (cooked and warmed)
16 anchovy fillets (rinsed and dried)
8   poached eggs
½   cup chopped cooked ham (warm)
1   T. glace de viande or meat glaze *
8   slices truffles (optional)

— Hollandaise Sauce —

1. Clarify butter by slowly melting it in a small pan. Let stand until clear part can be drawn easily.
2. Meanwhile, put vinegar, water, onion and peppercorns in saucepan and cook over low heat until liquid is reduced to one teaspoon. Remove peppercorns and cool.
3. Add egg yolks, beating lightly.
4. Beating constantly with electric beater, add clarified butter drop by drop until emulsified, then add butter in slow stream. Add lemon juice and set aside.

5. Preheat broiler. Place artichoke hearts in baking pan; top each with two anchovy fillets and warm briefly under broiler.
6. Top each with a poached egg; cover with Hollandaise sauce; sprinkle with chopped ham and a few drops of glace de viande.
7. Top with a truffle, if desired, and serve.

— Continued —

Serves: 4 for dinner, 8 for brunch
Preparation: 45 minutes

A favorite for someone who enjoys anchovies.

* Available at your meat market or in specialty food sections at grocer (ask the butcher). Two brand names are: BV and Magi. This glaze is simply beef stock cooked for many hours until it is reduced to a thick and highly potent concentrate. It must be used sparingly so as not to overpower a dish.

Chicken Creole

A LA - Antoine's

1	3½ lb. frying chicken (disjointed and cleaned)
¼	cup olive oil
1	lb. can tomatoes
2	T. butter (divided)
1	t. salt
	pepper
	cayenne
1	sprig thyme (or 1 t.)
1	T. parsley (minced)
1	bay leaf
3	garlic cloves (minced)
1	T. flour
6	shallots (chopped or ½ cup onions minced)
5	T. green pepper (chopped)
½	cup white wine

1. Saute chicken pieces in olive oil, browning on both sides. Remove from pan.
2. Add tomatoes and one tablespoon butter and simmer for ten minutes, stirring occasionally.
3. Add salt, a few grains of pepper and a dash of cayenne. Simmer for an additional ten minutes.
4. Add thyme, parsley, bay leaf and garlic. Simmer for fifteen minutes or until sauce is thick.
5. In a separate pan, melt remaining one tablespoon of butter; stir in flour and cook until it is brown. Add shallots and bell pepper and brown slightly. Add wine, stirring constantly until slightly thickened.
6. Combine wine sauce, tomato sauce and chicken in large pan. Cover and simmer forty five minutes or until chicken is tender.
7. Serve with steamed rice.

— Continued —

Serves: 4 - 6
Preparation: 15 minutes
Cooking: 1 hour 20 minutes

Delicious! Seasoned just right!

Pompano en Papillote

Begin day before or early in day.

A LA - Antoine's

6	medium sized pompano fillets (or any white fish fillet)
1	chopped shallot (or 2 T. chopped onion)
6	T. butter (divided)
2	cups white wine
1	cup crabmeat
1	cup shrimp (diced, cooked)
½	clove garlic (minced)
1½	cups onions (chopped)
	pinch thyme
1	bay leaf
2	cups fish stock *
2	T. flour
2	egg yolks
	salt (to taste)
	pepper (to taste)
6	pieces parchment paper (cut into hearts 12" long by 8" wide)

1. Saute fillets and shallots in two tablespoons melted butter. Add two cups wine and cover. Simmer until fillets are tender, approximately five - eight minutes. Drain, reserving liquid.
2. Saute crabmeat, shrimp and one-fourth clove garlic in two tablespoons butter. Add onions and remaining garlic and cook ten minutes.
3. Add thyme, bay leaf, one and three-fourths cups fish stock and simmer ten minutes.
4. In a separate pan, melt remaining butter, blend in flour and stir in remaining fish stock gradually.
5. Add to crabmeat along with liquid reserved from fillets.

— Continued —

6. Simmer, stirring constantly, until thickened.
7. Beat eggs; add to crabmeat. Add salt and pepper to taste. Chill in refrigerator until very firm (four or more hours).
8. Preheat oven to 450°.
9. Oil parchment paper well. Divide sauce into six portions.
10. Place one portion of sauce on one side of each heart. Lay fillet on top and fold over with other half of paper.
11. Seal edges of paper by folding over and pinching together all around.
12. Lay sealed hearts on oiled baking sheets.
13. Bake for fifteen minutes or until hearts are browned.
14. Serve at once, cutting open at the table.

Serves: 6
Preparation: 1½ hours
Baking: 15 minutes
Refrigeration: 4 hours (or more)

Delicious and worth extra effort.

* You can purchase bouillon cubes or see recipe in Glossary to make yourself.

Shrimp Mariniere

A LA - Antoine's

1½	lbs. raw shrimp (peeled and deveined)
2	cups white wine
2	minced shallots or ¼ cup minced onions
1	cup oyster water, fish stock or chicken stock
2	T. butter
2	T. flour
	juice of ¼ lemon
2	egg yolks (beaten)
½	cup light cream
1	T. parsley (chopped)

1. Combine wine, shallots and oyster water; bring to a boil; add shrimp and simmer fifteen minutes. Strain shrimp. Reserve wine-stock.
2. In a separate large pan, melt butter and blend in flour. Slowly add three quarters cup of the wine-stock combination, stirring constantly until thickened. Add shrimp; cook ten minutes and add lemon juice.
3. Combine egg yolks and cream; gradually add to shrimp mixture, stirring constantly.
4. Serve on toast points or in ramekins.

Serves: 4 - 6
Preparation: 10 minutes
Cooking: 35 minutes

Very good—doesn't mask shrimp.

Cafe Brûlot Diabolique

A LA - Antoine's

1	**stick cinnamon (1" long)**
8	**whole cloves**
	peel of 1 lemon (cut thin)
3	**lumps of sugar**
3	**jiggers brandy (warmed)**
3	**cups strong black coffee (hot)**

1. In a brûlot bowl, chafing dish or saucepan, place cinnamon, cloves, lemon peel and sugar.
2. Put brandy into a ladle; ignite*, and pour over ingredients in pan. Continue to ladle over ingredients until sugar dissolves.
3. Gradually add coffee and continue ladling mixture until flames fade.
4. Serve immediately in demitasse or brûlot cups.

Cooking: 8 minutes
Serves: 8 demitasse cups

"Flashy" after dinner drink!

* See Glossary of Terms.

Portrait Artists in Jackson Square

Beulah Ledner's Bakery

General Mills need not have gone to Madison Avenue to find Betty Crocker. The wholesomeness and trust this woman's visage is meant to impart can be found in New Orleans' own Beulah Ledner. With a smile sweetened by more than eighty years of living in a world of milk, honey, flour, shortening and sugar, Beulah has supplied New Orleans with quality pastries since the 1930's.

Operating initially out of her own kitchen, premium pastries, family support and good business sense necessitated expanding several times. At one time she employed a team of four bakers, four icing girls, a helper, a porter and six sales ladies in her modern, well-equipped bakery located near Fat City.

The pastries range from a vast array of small butter cookies to a three hundred pound wedding cake. In between, there are the popular Bavarian creams, European fruit cake slices, the date-nut and pecan cake, maple pecan cakes, chiffon sponge cakes and one of Beulah's own creations— *The Doberage Cake* which features a butter cake dough, with custard filling in four flavors.

— Continued —

21

Specialty cakes are frequently seen on the frosting table. The huge *Hamburger Cake* dwarfs a hundred Big Whoppers and a moist and tasty replica of a pair of glasses was the spectacle at a celebration for an opthalmologist.

Beulah is not one of those who is content to sit at home and crochet while awaiting visits from her two children, five grandchildren and three great grandchildren. She drives her car to work six days a week, is there by 9:00 A.M. and works a full day. She should be an inspiration to all of us, particularly senior citizens who may sense a loss of life's purpose.

Since the first printing of this book, Mrs. Ledner has retired. Since her recipes are so popular, we've kept them in A La New Orleans for your enjoyment.

Date, Rum and Pecan Cake

A LA Beulah Ledner's Bakery

— Cake —

1	cup granulated sugar	2	t. baking powder
1	cup brown sugar	1½	t. vanilla
4	whole eggs		ground rind of ½
¾	lb. chopped dates		orange and ½ lemon
1	cup pecan pieces		juice of ½ orange
1½	t. cinnamon		and ½ lemon
1	t. allspice	3	oz. rum
2	cups sifted flour		

— Icing —

2	T. butter (softened)	1	t. vanilla
1	cup powdered sugar	½	cup chopped pecans
2	T. rum		

— Cake —

1. Combine all cake ingredients in a large bowl and mix well.
2. Pour into a greased 9 X 13" pan.
3. Bake in 350° oven for thirty minutes.
4. Remove and cool on rack.

— Icing —

5. Cream butter and sugar together. Add rum and vanilla and beat till smooth.
6. When cake is cool, spread with icing and sprinkle with pecans.

Preparation: 20 minutes
Baking: 30 minutes
Serves: 8 - 10

A tasty tea cake or light dessert.

Fresh Fruit Kuchen *

A LA Beulah Ledner's Bakery

— Cake —

1	cup flour	1	egg
1	t. baking powder	2	T. butter
¼	t. salt	2	T. milk
2	T. sugar		

4   T. butter (melted)
2   lbs. or more fresh fruit such as peeled peaches, apples or prune plums (sliced)

— Custard —

1   whole egg
½   cup milk
⅛   t. salt

— Topping —

¼	cup brown sugar	1	t. cinnamon
¼	cup granulated sugar	¼	cup butter
1	T. flour	¼	cup pecans (chopped)

1. Preheat oven to 350°.
2. Combine all cake ingredients, mixing well. Spread on bottom of buttered 9 X 13" pan. Brush dough with melted butter.
3. Top dough with sliced fresh fruit; spread evenly and fairly thick.

— Continued —

— Custard —

4.   Beat together custard ingredients and pour over fruit.

5.   Blend together topping ingredients and cover top evenly.
6.   Bake in oven for ½ to ¾ hour until brown. Serve hot or cold
     in square portions.

Preparation: 30 minutes
Baking: 30 minutes
Serves: 8

Delicious—not too rich.

*"A delightful dessert for luncheons, dinners and coffee parties."

A LA Beulah Ledner's Bakery

— Cake —

½	lb. butter	1	t. vanilla
¾	cup sugar	3	cups cake flour
3	egg yolks (save whites)	½	t. baking powder

1   cup preserves (strawberry or raspberry)
½   cup bread crumbs
1   cup pecans (chopped)

— Meringue —

3   egg whites
     pinch of salt
3   T. sugar

¼   cup ground pecans

— Cake —

1. Preheat oven to 325°.
2. Cream butter and sugar well; add egg yolks and vanilla.
3. Combine flour and baking powder; add to creamed mixture and mix well.
4. Spread with fingertips in a buttered 9 X 13" pan.
5. Cover with preserves; sprinkle with bread crumbs, then pecans.

— Meringue —

6. Beat egg whites, salt and sugar to a stiff consistency.

— Continued —

7.   Spread meringue over mixture in pan and sprinkle meringue with ground pecans.
8.   Bake in 325° oven one hour. Remove. Cool well and cut into narrow, oblong slices.

Yield: 3 dozen
Preparation: 30 minutes
Baking: 1 hour

A delicious cookie for desserts or snacking!

A New Orleans Jazz Band

Le Bon Creole

Located in the French Quarter, the Maison Dupuy Hotel and its restaurant — Le Bon Creole are a class act. Both exude a polished look from the facilities to the personnel and overlook the regal courtyard which contains the beautiful Fountain of the Arts.

The interior decor is soft sophistication. Shades of saffron are created by the combination of cypress paneling, ceiling lamps and soft candlelight. French doors dominate one wall and open onto the courtyard and romantic fountain. Royal blue drapes, powder blue tablecloths and fresh carnations complete the setting.

— Continued —

Authentic cajun and creole cooking are available at breakfast, lunch and dinner. Luncheon and dinner menus offer a choice of a la carte or table d'hote. Fresh seafoods include Speckled Trout, Red Snapper, Redfish, Pompano, freshwater Blue Channel Catfish, Shellfish and Maine Lobster. Steaks, Rack of Lamb, Veal, Quail and Frog legs are also available. The *Crabmeat, Shrimp* and *Crawfish Etouffees* are popular entrees. The secret of the cajun cooking at Le Bon Creole is the delicate blending of herbs and spices, cooked over a low flame. To complement any entree, an unusually fine selection of wines is available.

Luncheon specials are available on weekdays. Monday traditionally calls for *Red Beans and Rice with Cajun Sausage*. Breakfast includes *Lost Bread*, omelettes, classical egg dishes, breakfast steaks and porkchops.

Stuffed Mushrooms
(hors d'oeuvre)

A LA - Le Bon Creole

1	**large onion (chopped)**
1	**bell pepper (chopped)**
2	**stalks celery (chopped)**
1	**clove garlic (chopped)**
2	**T. salad oil**
1	**cup toasted day old bread crumbs**
½	**lb. chopped boiled shrimp**
½	**lb. lump crabmeat (cooked)**
½	**t. parsley**
1	**egg**
	salt and pepper (to taste)
50	**mushroom caps (washed)**∗

1. Saute onion, pepper, celery and garlic in oil.
2. Soak bread in ½ cup water to moisten, then squeeze out water.
3. Combine sauteed vegetables, bread, shrimp, crab, parsley and egg. Mix well and season to taste.
4. Stuff mushroom caps with one teaspoon of mixture; broil until brown and warm through.

Yields: 50 hors d'oeuvres
Preparation: 25 minutes
Cooking/Baking: 10 minutes/3-4 minutes

∗ Author's Note: If you'd like you may use your imagination and use the stuffing for other vegetables or on toast points, crackers, etc.

Crawfish Etouffee

A LA - Le Bon Creole

5   **lbs. live crawfish** OR **2 lbs. shrimp** (cooked, cleaned, deveined)
2   **cups fresh fish stock** *
4   **T. butter**
4   **T. flour**
1   **cup onions (finely chopped)**
1   **cup green onions, including green tops (finely chopped)**
½   **cup celery (finely chopped)**
1   **large clove garlic (finely chopped)**
1   **1 lb. can tomatoes (drained, finely chopped)**
1   **T. Worcestershire sauce**
¼   **t. cayenne (less if using shrimp)**
1   **t. black pepper (freshly ground)**
2   **t. salt**
4 - 6 **cups long grain white rice (cooked)**

Omit steps one - three if using shrimp.

1. Soak the live crawfish in cold water for at least ten minutes and wash thoroughly under cold running water. In a heavy eight to ten quart pot, bring four quarts of water to a boil over high heat. Using tongs, drop in crawfish and boil briskly, uncovered, for five minutes.
2. Drain the crawfish in a large colander. When they are cool enough to handle, shell them one at a time in the following manner. With your hands, break off the ridged tail, snap it in half lengthwise and lift out the meat in one piece. If you like, you can snap off the large claws, break them with a nutcracker and pick out the bits of claw meat.

— Continued —

3. Some or all of the yellow fat or "butter" from the body of the crawfish may slide out when you break off the tail. If it does not, scoop the shell clean with the tip of one thumb and pick out the yellow fat. Reserve the crawfish meat and fat (there will be about two cups). Discard the shells, heads and intestinal matter.

4. Bring fish stock to a boil over high heat. Remove and keep covered and warm.

5. Meanwhile, in a five to six quart stock pan melt four table-spoons of butter; stir in flour and blend over very low heat. Continue cooking, stirring occasionally, until the roux becomes golden brown in color, about twenty minutes.

6. Add onions, green onions, celery and garlic. Cook over moderate heat until soft, approximately five minutes.

7. While stirring, pour in fish stock in slow steady stream. Stir constantly until mixture boils and thickens slightly.

8. Add tomatoes, Worcestershire, cayenne, black pepper and salt. Reduce heat to low and simmer, partially covered, for thirty minutes.

9. Stir in crawfish tails and butter fat OR shrimp and cook until thoroughly heated.

10. Taste for seasoning. Serve in heated bowl accompanied by rice.

Serves: 4 - 6
Preparation: Crawfish: 3 hours; Shrimp: 1 hour

Chef says this dish prepared with live crawfish is rich and thick. When prepared with shrimp it is good but lacks the richness of the crawfish fat. "Etouffee literally means 'smothered,' and in this dish the crawfish tails are blanketed with a rich, thick sauce."

* See Glossary of Terms.

Horse Drawn Carriage in the French Quarter

BON TON

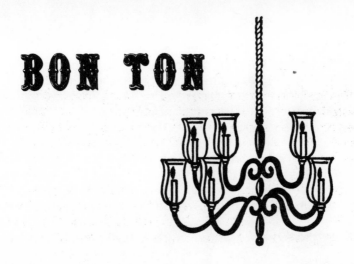

Crawfish, crayfish, crawdads, creekcrabs and yabbies are all one and the same. From December to July they are gathered from Louisiana's lakes and rivers and restaurant menus take on an added gloss.

One such establishment is the Bon Ton. To an already formidable array of entrees is added a variety of crawfish dishes that include crawfish bisque, omelettes, jambalaya, fried crawfish tails, crawfish newburg and crawfish etouffee.

Owner Alvin Pierce brought his cajun cooking techniques into the kitchen in 1953 and no one has regretted his decision. Mr. Pierce describes much of his food as "southwest Louisiana type" as in Acadiana, the bayou, where cooking is simple, for the ribs as well as the soul.

The palate should also find satisfaction with the Bon Ton's homemade soup and homemade seafood gumbo. There is fried and broiled shrimp, oysters and softshell crab. Several other restaurant owners extolled the virtues of the Bon Ton's version of bread pudding with whiskey sauce.

— Continued —

At the Bon Ton everything is thought of as a "special" and is treated as such during the entire preparatory process. Foods are cooked in their own juices and fresh seasonings are the rule. A staff of seven cooks were taught from scratch by Mr. Pierce to prevent their acquiring any bad habits.

The Bon Ton is located in a former warehouse which was built in 1845. The original brick walls and lintels remain. The interior offers a "Delmonico look" with its exposed brick, shuttered windows, high ceiling, dark rafters and red checkered tablecloths.

Reservations are suggested for the evening meal.

Shrimp Etouffee

A LA - The Bon Ton

parsley-buttered rice *
4   **T. butter**
4   **cups small shrimp (shelled and cleaned)**
1   **t. garlic (chopped finely)**
    salt and pepper
4   **t. parsley (chopped)**

1. Have prepared: rice for four, buttered and sprinkled with parsley. Keep hot.*
2. Melt butter in saucepan; add shrimp, garlic salt and pepper. Cook ten minutes. Add parsley.
3. Serve over parsley-buttered rice.

Serves: 4
Preparation: 5 minutes (does not include rice preparation).
Cooking: 12 minutes

Very easy dish to make.

Shrimp and Oyster Jambalaya

A LA - The Bon Ton

2	cups cooked rice
½	cup shortening
3	large white onions (chopped)
3	bell peppers (chopped)
3	stems of celery (chopped)
1	t. garlic (chopped)
2	small cans tomato paste
4	doz. medium shrimp (shelled)
4	doz. oysters (shelled)

1. Cook rice according to package directions. Keep warm.
2. Meanwhile, melt shortening; add onions, peppers, celery, garlic and saute. Add tomato paste and simmer 1½ hours.
3. Add shrimp and cook ten minutes. Add oysters and cook an additional ten minutes.
4. Combine with the rice and serve immediately.

Preparation: 30 minutes
Cooking: 1½ hours
Serves: 6 - 8

Very good entree!

Chicken Stew

A LA - The Bon Ton

1	chicken (cut up)
	salt and pepper
	flour
	shortening
¾	cup butter or margarine
¾	cup flour
1	white onion (chopped)
1	bell pepper (chopped)
2	ribs celery (chopped)
½	t. garlic (chopped)

1. Sprinkle chicken pieces with salt and pepper and flour lightly.
2. Brown chicken in melted shortening. Remove from heat.
3. In separate pot make a roux by melting butter and slowly adding flour. Cook over low heat until it is a thick paste, approximately five minutes.
4. Put 1½ quarts water in large soup pot. Add chicken roux and stir to mix. Add vegetables and garlic and cook about one hour or until chicken is tender.

Serves: 4
Preparation: 10 minutes
Cooking: 1 hour 20 minutes

A LA - The Bon Ton

3	medium eggplants	½	lb. lump crabmeat
¼	cup margarine	¼	cup parsley
2	bell peppers (chopped)	½	cup bread crumbs
2	med. onions (chopped)		salt & pepper (to taste)
¼	cup celery (chopped)		paprika
1	clove garlic (minced)	3	T. vegetable oil
½	lb. small shrimp (peeled and deveined)		

1. Boil whole eggplants in enough water to cover, until soft, approximately twenty minutes. When cool enough to handle, cut in half lengthwise.
2. Scoop out meat of eggplants, being careful not to pierce shells. Reserve shells and chop meat.
3. Melt margarine in large skillet and saute peppers, onions, celery and garlic until limp, about ten minutes.
4. Add chopped eggplant meat and simmer until water has evaporated.
5. Mix in shrimp and cook an additional twenty minutes.
6. Put shrimp mixture in a large bowl and fold in crabmeat and parsley.
7. Preheat oven to 350°. Cool mixture slightly. Add one quarter cup or more bread crumbs to firm up mixture. Salt and pepper to taste.
8. Stuff eggplant shells and sprinkle tops lightly with additional bread crumbs and paprika.
9. Brush tops very lightly with oil and bake in oven for thirty minutes.

— Continued —

Stuffed Eggplant — Continued

Serves: 6
Preparation: 1 hour
Baking: 30 minutes

For stuffed eggplant lovers—a must!

Bread Pudding with Whiskey Sauce
(Begin several hours ahead or day before)

A LA - The Bon Ton

1	loaf French bread	2	T. vanilla
1	qt. milk	1	cup raisins
3	eggs (beaten)	3	T. margarine
2	cups sugar		

— Whiskey Sauce —

¼	lb. butter or margarine
1	cup confectioner's sugar
1	egg (well beaten)
2	T. whiskey (more to taste)

1. Preheat oven to 350°. Break bread apart into four pieces. In large bowl, soak bread in milk; mash with fingers until well mixed.
2. Add eggs, sugar, vanilla and raisins; stir well.
3. Grease a thick pan with margarine; pour in pudding. Place pan in a shallow pan which has one inch boiling water in it. Bake in oven for about forty-five minutes, until very firm.
4. Allow to cool.

— Whiskey Sauce —

5. In a double boiler, cook butter and sugar until well dissolved and very hot.
6. Add egg, whipping very fast, so that it won't curdle.
7. When very smooth, remove from heat and chill. Add whiskey to taste.

— Continued —

8. When ready to serve, cut pudding into cubes and place in individual, oven-proof dishes. Top with some of the sauce and heat under broiler.
9. Serve with additional whiskey sauce.

Serves: 6
Preparation: 30 minutes
Baking: 45 minutes

A good bread pudding!

Brennan's Courtyard

A person seeking to experience the best in New Orleans cuisine, along with handsome settings traditionally associated with the City, would do well to dine at Brennan's. Located at 417 Royal Street, the restaurant showcases a man, an idea, years of hard work and now widespread fame. Unfortunately Owen Brennan did not live to see the more than twenty "Holiday" awards that line the restaurant's upper corridors. However, Owen Brennan's exuberance is recaptured daily on the faces of the more than fourteen hundred patrons who enter this historical address for breakfast, lunch and dinner. It is Sunday seven days a week at Brennan's and placidity is left at the door. A controlled fervor resides amidst the canopied foyer, circular stairway, handsome dining areas and verdant patio that accommodates patrons sipping creamy drinks prior to seating.

— Continued —

Brennan's did not win its laurels on atmosphere, decor, and delicious drinks. Inventive meals, prepared with quality ingredients and consistent skill, are served throughout the day. Breakfast and brunch feature famous egg dishes like *Eggs St. Charles*, a presentation of poached eggs on fried trout topped with hollandaise. *Eggs Sardou* consists of poached eggs over creamed spinach and artichoke bottoms with the popular hollandaise providing the final complement. Lunch and dinner offer a variety of entrees like the *Chicken Kottwitz*, a sauteed chicken breast with fresh mushrooms, diced artichoke bottoms and lemon-butter sauce. Desserts are served at all meals and include sauteed bananas flamed in rum with a banana liqueur and spices, all served over vanilla ice cream. They call it *Bananas Foster* and it's a palatal pancea. All meals can be ordered a la carte or table d'hote.

Brennan's is open daily, and reservations are advised.

Eggs a la Nouvelle Orleans

A LA Brennan's

2	cups water	8	large eggs
¼	cup dry white wine	2	T. butter
¼	t. salt	¾	lb. crabmeat

— Brandy Cream Sauce—

½	cup butter	¼	t. salt
¾	cup flour		pinch black pepper
2	cups milk	1	T. brandy

1. Bring water, wine and salt to a continuous low rolling boil, in large skillet or pan. Crack eggs and add one at a time. Poach until whites are firm, about two minutes. Lift out with slotted spoon and place on heated platter. Keep warm.
2. Melt butter in skillet over low heat. Add crabmeat and cook until just heated through, about five minutes.

— Brandy Cream Sauce —

3. Melt butter in saucepan over low heat. Gradually stir in flour and cook two minutes, stirring constantly. Slowly pour in milk continuing to stir until sauce thickens to medium consistency. Season with salt, pepper and brandy.
4. Assemble the dish by placing three ounces crabmeat on each plate. Top each with two eggs and ladle sauce over all. Serve immediately.

Serves: 4
Preparation: 30 minutes

An elegant brunch or luncheon dish! Yummy!

Onion Soup

A LA Brennan's

¾　cup butter
2　cups yellow onions (thinly sliced)
1　cup (less 2 T.) flour
1½　quarts beef stock (not beef bouillon) *
½　T. Worcestershire
　salt (to taste)
　white pepper (to taste)
1　T. heavy cream
　croutons
　Parmesan cheese (grated)

1. In a soup kettle, melt butter over medium heat. Add onions and reduce heat to very low. Cook onion until just tender but not brown.
2. Stir in flour and cook ten minutes longer, stirring occasionally.
3. Add stock, Worcestershire, salt and pepper. Stir to mix. Raise heat and bring to a boil. Lower heat and simmer about fifteen minutes.
4. Remove kettle from heat and stir in heavy cream.
5. Serve garnished with croutons and Parmesan cheese.

Serves: 4 - 6
Cooking: 35 minutes

Good soup!

* Beef bouillon tends to be too salty.

Potato Salad

A LA Brennan's

6-7	white potatoes
2	stalks celery (finely chopped)
½	medium white onion (finely chopped)
¼	small green pepper (finely chopped)
8-10	pimiento-stuffed olives (finely chopped)
4	hard boiled eggs (3 finely chopped, 1 sliced)
¼	cup olive oil
⅓	cup red wine vinegar with garlic
1	or more T. mayonnaise
1	t. salt
⅓	t. black pepper
	sprigs of parsley for garnish

1. Boil potatoes in skins for about one hour or until tender. Drain water and let potatoes cool until they are cool enough to handle. Peel and slice one-eighth inch thick.
2. Put potatoes in serving bowl; add chopped vegetables, olives and three chopped eggs.
3. Pour olive oil and vinegar over all and mix gently to distribute evenly. Add mayonnaise, salt and pepper and mix. (More mayonnaise may be added according to taste).
4. Arrange sliced egg and parsley sprigs over top to decorate. Cover and refrigerate, if not served immediately.

Serves: 8
Preparation: 25 minutes
Cooking: 1 hour

Lump Crabmeat Owen with Thousand Island Dressing

A LA Brennan's

— Thousand Island Dressing —

2	cups mayonnaise
1½	cups chili sauce
3	hard boiled eggs (finely chopped)
1	dill pickle (finely chopped)
2	T. parsley (finely chopped)
1	T. pimento (finely chopped)
2	T. Worcestershire sauce
16	leaves romaine lettuce (rinsed, dried & crisped in the refrigerator)
3	lbs. crabmeat

— Dressing —

1. Combine first seven ingredients in a bowl and blend thoroughly.
2. Cover bowl and chill completely before using.

3. To serve, arrange two leaves of lettuce on each plate. Top with one eighth of crabmeat and spoon one third cup dressing over crab.

Preparation: 10 minutes
Refrigeration: 1 hour
Serves: 8

Delicious—a rich dish!

Veal Jason

A LA Brennan's

12	3 oz. medallions of veal (pounded ⅛" thick)
	salt and pepper
3	eggs (lightly beaten)
1½	cups seasoned bread crumbs
½	cup butter

— Sauce —

3	T. butter
1½	cups sour cream
½	cup catsup
2	T. lemon juice
2	t. Worcestershire sauce

1. Lightly season veal medallions with salt and pepper. Dip veal in egg and thoroughly cover with bread crumbs.
2. Melt butter in large skillet. Sauté veal until golden brown, approximately 8 - 10 minutes. Remove and keep warm.

— Sauce —

3. Melt butter in saucepan. Blend in remaining ingredients and simmer over very low heat for five minutes.
4. Serve veal with sauce.

Serves: 6
Cooking: 15 minutes

Delicious and quick!

Bananas Foster

A LA Brennan's

4   **T. butter**
3½ **T. brown sugar**
½   **t. cinnamon**
2   **T. banana liqueur**
4   **bananas (cut in half lengthwise, then halved)**
¼   **cup rum (approximately)**
4   **scoops vanilla ice cream**

1. Melt butter in a flambe pan or attractive skillet. Add sugar, cinnamon, banana liqueur and stir to mix.
2. Heat for a few minutes; place banana quarters in sauce and saute until soft and slightly browned.
3. Add rum and allow to heat. Ignite.* Allow sauce to flame until it dies out, tipping pan in circular motion to prolong flaming.
4. Place ice cream in individual bowls. Cover with four pieces of banana. Spoon hot sauce over top and serve immediately.

Serves: 4
Cooking: 8 - 10 minutes

One of Brennan's most popular desserts and very easy to duplicate at home.

*See Glossary of Terms (Let rum get hot so you get a good flame when it's ignited).

Hot Spiced Apples with Double Cream

A LA Brennan's

8   firm red apples
3   T. sugar
1½   t. cinnamon
2⅔   cups heavy cream

1. Preheat oven to 400°.
2. Wash, dry and core apples.
3. Place in shallow baking dish. Sprinkle with sugar and cinnamon and bake for fifty minutes.
4. Remove from oven and place in eight heated bowls. Pour one third cup cream over each portion and serve immediately.

Preparation: 10 minutes
Baking 50 minutes
Serves: 8

Absinthe Suissesse *

A LA Brennan's

6	oz. absinthe (Pernod, Ricard)
2	large egg whites
1	cup heavy cream
2	oz. Orgeat syrup
1	cup crushed ice

1. Place all ingredients into blender and blend on high speed.
2. Serve in old fashioned glasses.

Serves: 4
Preparation: 5 minutes

*A good after dinner drink.

Milk Punch

A LA Brennan's

¾ **cup bourbon**
1½ **cups half and half**
1 **oz. simple syrup***
6 **drops vanilla extract**
ice cubes
nutmeg

1. Combine all ingredients, except nutmeg, in cocktail shaker.
2. Shake vigorously; strain into old fashioned glasses.
3. Sprinkle each drink with nutmeg before serving.

Serves: 4
Preparation: 8 minutes

*See recipe page 56.

Ramos Gin Fizz

A LA Brennan's

— Simple Syrup —

¼   cup sugar
1   cup hot water

— Gin Fizz —

6   oz. gin
1½   oz. simple syrup
2   large egg whites
½   t. orange flower water
1½   cups heavy cream
1   cup crushed ice

— Simple Syrup —

1. Prepare simple syrup by combining sugar and water, stirring constantly until sugar melts.

— Gin Fizz —

2. Combine remaining ingredients in blender and blend together on high speed for thirty seconds (turning on and off again) until frothy.
3. Serve in old fashioned glasses.

Serves: 4
Preparation: 10 minutes

Comment: Good brunch drink. Simple syrup keeps in refrigerator indefinitely.

Sazerac

A LA Brennan's

2	t. Pernod
6	oz. bourbon
1	oz. simple syrup (see page 56)
12	drops Angostura bitters
12	drops Peychaud bitters
8	ice cubes
4	lemon twists

1. Pour one half teaspoon Pernod into each of four old fashioned glasses.
2. Turn glasses to coat inside surfaces evenly. Pour off excess and discard.
3. Combine remaining ingredients in cocktail shaker or pitcher.
4. Stir to mix; strain into glasses.
5. Serve garnished with lemon twists.

Serves: 4
Preparation: 10 minutes

The Cornstalk House - famous for the "Cornstalk Fence"

Caribbean Room

An illuminating fact regarding the Caribbean Room is that a major portion of its clientele are residents of New Orleans. This award winning restaurant, situated in the famous Pontchartrain Hotel, has been attracting capacity crowds since the late 1940's. Through the years, Lysle Aschaffenburg, founder of both this famous restaurant and luxury hotel, has successfully maintained kitchen staffs imbued in the ways of traditional New Orleans cooking.

On a Thursday evening, I found the Caribbean Room alive with conversive patrons, attentive waiters and Chef Louis Evans welcoming diners and encouraging unreserved comments on the food and its presentation. My dinner consisted of a vintage Chablis from the well-stocked wine cellar, the popular *Shrimp Saki*, the delicious *Oyster Broth*, *Red Fish Pontchartrain*, a baked potato stuffed with cheddar cheese, a cooked tomato stuffed with spinach and finally, the *Pecan Snowball* which features vanilla ice cream, The Ponchartrain's famous chocolate sauce, sliced pecans and shredded coconut. I was at a loss to provide Chef Evans with any criticisms.

— Continued —

I found the Sunday buffet an equally well attended affair. A deluxe roasted Prime Rib presided over a long table which included other meat dishes, shrimp, crabmeat, vegetables, cheeses, elegant fruit and vegetable molds, a large punch bowl containing sliced fresh fruits in their natural juices, along with homemade brownies and *Southern Pecan Pie*. There awaits an added treat for those who dare — The Pontchartrain's famous *Mile High Ice Cream Pie* — a Brobdingnagian dessert creation consisting of several types of ice cream, a meringue and the exquisite chocolate sauce.

Reservations are suggested.

Oyster Broth

A LA - The Caribbean Room

1	white onion (chopped)
2	ribs celery (chopped)
½	lb. butter
¼	cup flour
2	quarts water
2	quarts oysters
2	bay leaves
	salt and pepper (to taste)
	parsley for garnish

1. Saute onion and celery in butter; do not brown.
2. Stir in flour.
3. Add water, oysters and bay leaves.
4. Bring to a boil; reduce heat and simmer for ten minutes.
5. Strain. Salt and pepper to taste.
6. Garnish with parsley and serve.

Serves: 10
Preparation: 40 minutes

Rich and delicious—a subtle oyster flavor.

Oyster Broth

A LA - The Caribbean Room

1	white onion (chopped)
2	ribs celery (chopped)
½	lb. butter
¼	cup flour
2	quarts water
2	quarts oysters
2	bay leaves
	salt and pepper (to taste)
	parsley for garnish

1. Saute onion and celery in butter; do not brown.
2. Stir in flour.
3. Add water, oysters and bay leaves.
4. Bring to a boil; reduce heat and simmer for ten minutes.
5. Strain. Salt and pepper to taste.
6. Garnish with parsley and serve.

Serves: 10
Preparation: 40 minutes

Rich and delicious—a subtle oyster flavor.

Creole Seafood Gumbo
(Begin several hours ahead)

A LA - The Caribbean Room

½	lb. large shrimp (in shells)
3	T. shortening
3	T. flour
½	green pepper (chopped)
1	stalk celery (chopped)
1	small onion (chopped)
1	large or 2 small crabs (cleaned and shells removed)
2	T. butter
1	t. pepper
1	t. thyme
1	T. salt
1	T. Worchestershire sauce
1	bay leaf
	pinch of cayenne
½	cup canned tomatoes (chopped)
½	cup canned okra (finely chopped)

1. Peel shrimp and boil hulls in four cups of water for one hour. Strain broth or liquor from hulls and save.
2. Heat shortening and slowly stir in flour to make a roux. Cook until roux is dark brown.
3. Add vegetables and cook, stirring constantly, until moisture is reduced.
4. Saute shrimp and crabmeat in butter. Add to roux. Add seasonings.
5. Pour shrimp liquor into roux; stir. Add tomatoes and bring to a boil.
6. Reduce heat and simmer two to two and one half hours.
7. Add okra; cook another twenty minutes until gumbo is thick.

Serves: 10
Preparation: 4 hours

Can be frozen if desired.

Oysters en Brochette

A LA - The Caribbean Room

½   lb. bacon (cut in 2" strips)
3   dozen fresh oysters
2   cups flour
4-6 T. solid shortening
4   tomato halves (broiled)
4   lemon wedges
4   sprigs parsley

1. Fry bacon until transparent but not crisp. Remove and drain.
2. On 4 (10 inch) skewers, alternate pieces of bacon and oysters, using approximately nine oysters per skewer.
3. Dredge brochettes in flour until well coated, shake off excess.
4. Saute brochettes in melted shortening until crisp on outside and golden brown.
5. Remove from pan and place on plate. Slide out skewer and garnish with tomato, lemon and parsley.

Serves: 4
Preparation: 20 minutes
Cooking: 25 minutes

A must for oyster lovers!

Trout Eugene

A LA - The Caribbean Room

¼	cup butter	32	small shrimp
4	fillets of trout		(cleaned & deveined)
¼	cup butter	¼	cup butter
8	oz. crabmeat	2	t. Worcestershire sauce
4	T. shallots	2	t. lemon juice

1. In a skillet with melted butter, saute trout until nicely browned (approximately five to eight minutes). Remove from pan and keep warm.
2. In same skillet with melted butter, cook crabmeat and shallots, stirring gently, until shallots are tender.
3. In another pan cook shrimp in butter. Add Worcestershire sauce and lemon juice.
4. To serve, place trout fillet on plate; top with crabmeat at one end and shrimp at the other.

Serves: 4
Preparation: 20 minutes

A fantastic flavor combination. Very easy to prepare.

A LA - The Caribbean Room

1½	lbs. shrimp in shells
½	qt. shrimp stock *
2	green onions (chopped)
3	large fresh mushrooms (sliced)
4	oz. butter
½	cup flour
2	T. sherry wine
2	T. white wine
¼	cup half and half
	salt and pepper (to taste)
8	flaky pastry shells (optional)

1. Clean and devein shrimp. Save hulls and set aside shrimp.
2. Simmer clean shrimp hulls in two and one half cups water for thirty minutes. Strain and save stock. *
3. Boil shrimp in stock about five minutes or until pink. Set aside.
4. Saute green onions and mushrooms in butter for approximately five to eight minutes. Add flour; cook five more minutes, stirring constantly.
5. Slowly add shrimp, stock, sherry and wine.
6. Heat cream and slowly add to shrimp mixture.
7. Add salt and pepper. Cook on low for fifteen minutes until thick, stirring often.
8. Serving suggestion: Serve in a flaky pastry shell with buttered green asparagus.

Serves: 4 - 5
Preparation: 45 minutes

Excellent dish!

In the kitchen of Chez Helene they are squeezing blood from the proverbial turnip. More specifically, how is it that a kitchen, so comparatively small, can produce so much that is so good in so many different ways?

Several facts were related to me as I sought an unoccupied corner in the kitchen and momentarily recalled a childhood visit aboard a captured submarine. Chez Helene's is a black, family-owned and operated restaurant. It serves breakfast, lunch and dinner seven days a week. The availability of *Oysters Rockefeller, Trout Marguery,* as well as *Fried Chicken, Turnip Greens* and *Corn Bread* indicate the diversity of the menu.

The cuisine has been described as soul by some and creole by others. Austin Leslie, the founder's nephew, calls the cooking southern style. His recipes for *Stuffed Green Peppers* and *Bread Pudding* have filled a trophy room and tables alike. A gregarious man, Austin appreciates the importance of encouraging communication between the races and does his part by making all his customers feel equally at home in the two clean, but modest, dining rooms.

— Continued —

Helene Dejean Pollack spooned the first servings in this success story when she opened Howard's Eatery at a different location in 1942. Since then, brothers, sisters, nieces and nephews, under Helen's tutelage, have continued her reputation for good food in ample portions at reasonable prices.

Blacks have traditionally held some of the culinary world's most legendary ladles. An equally qualified ladle resides ten minutes by cab from the French Quarter on North Robertson.

Fried Chicken

A LA Chez Helene

2 •	fryers or broilers (cut up)
	salt and pepper
1	cup of evaporated milk
4	eggs
⅓	cup water
½	cup flour
	fat or cooking oil

1. Wash chicken pieces and pat dry. Sprinkle with salt and pepper.
2. In a medium sized bowl, combine evaporated milk, eggs and water; mix well.
3. Dip chicken pieces into above mixture. Dip into flour.
4. Fry in 1½ - 2 inches of fat or oil (about 350°) for approximately ten to fifteen minutes or until brown on all sides. To test for doneness, squeeze gently with tongs; if chicken is done the juice that runs out will show no trace of red.
5. Drain on absorbant paper.

Serves: 6
Preparation: 1 hour

Excellent recipe—chicken is very crisp!

Crabmeat Dressing *

A LA Chez Helene

¼   **lb. margarine**
2   **T. parsley (chopped)**
½   **large onion (chopped)**
½   **cup celery (chopped)**
1   **loaf stale French bread**
3   **eggs (beaten)**
1   **lb. crabmeat**
½   **t. thyme**
    salt and pepper (to taste)

1. Melt margarine in large skillet; add parsley, onion and celery. Simmer twenty minutes.
2. Meanwhile, break bread into small cubes and crumbs. Sprinkle with water in a large baking pan. Add eggs and mix thoroughly.
3. Cook crabmeat in margarine-onion mixture about ten minutes. Add to breadcrumbs and stir well.
4. Add thyme and salt and pepper.
5. Bake at 350° for two hours. Stir every thirty minutes.
6. After baking; cool in refrigerator. Dressing is now ready for further use — i.e. — stuffing for crab shells, shrimp or lobster. After stuffing, top with bread crumbs, melted margarine and brown under broiler. *

Serves: 5-6
Preparation: 40 minutes
Baking: 2 hours

Very good: has a wonderful crab taste!

Stuffed Bell Peppers

A LA Chez Helene

¼	lb. margarine	1	loaf stale French bread (crumbled)
1	small onion (finely chopped)	½	cup water
½	stalk celery (finely chopped)	3	eggs (lightly beaten) salt & pepper (to taste)
2	T. parsley (finely chopped)	½	t. thyme
1	lb. ground beef	3	bell peppers
1	lb. shrimp (peeled, deveined and coarsely chopped	¼	cup bread crumbs
		¼	cup margarine (melted)

1. Melt margarine in large skillet; slowly saute onion, celery and parsley for twenty minutes.
2. Preheat oven to 300°. Add ground beef and shrimp to onion mixture, stirring to break up meat. Cook for twenty minutes.
3. Place bread in large baking pan; moisten with water; add eggs and mix thoroughly. Add beef and shrimp mixture. Season with salt, pepper and thyme. Stir well.
4. Place pan in oven and bake for two hours, stirring well every half hour.
5. Remove from oven and cool in refrigerator.
6. Stuff pepper halves. Top with bread crumbs and melted margarine.
7. Brown under broiler. Serve immediately!

Serves: 4-6
Preparation: 50 minutes
Cooking: 20 minutes
Baking: 2 hours

Turnip Greens

A LA Chez Helene

4	**bunches of turnip greens (with the turnips) ***
¼	**lb. margarine**
1	**large onion (diced)**
1	**garlic clove (minced)**
¾	**lb. of ham shoulder (cooked, diced) ****
	salt and pepper (to taste)
	vinegar

1. Wash turnip greens in cold water; trim off blemished areas; remove leaves from stems.
2. Scrub turnips with a brush; scrape and pare. Leave small white turnips whole if desired. Slice or dice large ones.
3. Melt margarine in three or four quart saucepan. Add onion, garlic and ham and saute for about ten minutes. Add greens and turnips; cover pan and cook on low for two hours. Stir every half hour, being sure to get to the bottom of the pot. (There should be enough water from washing and cooking the greens to cook without burning). Taste for seasoning and add salt and pepper accordingly.
4. Serve. Have vinegar on the table so each person may add as much as he likes to this Southern dish. (see note)

Serves: 6
Preparation: 30 minutes
Cooking: 2 hours

* You may substitute any other greens you prefer. Remember they cook down to smaller amounts as with spinach.

** The original recipe calls for Pickle Tips which is available readily in New Orleans but harder to come by in other parts of the country. Pickle Tips are the tips of pork ribs cooked and pickled.

NOTE: In some Southern restaurants it's very common to have vinegar on the table with the salt and pepper. Be sure to use it, especially with this dish.

Red Beans

Begin night before.

A LA Chez Helene

½	**lb. red beans**
½	**lb. ham shoulder (chunked)**
1	**cup onion (finely chopped)**
1	**stalk celery (finely chopped)**
½	**bell pepper (finely chopped)**
1	**T. parsley**
⅛	**lb. margarine**
	salt and pepper (to taste)

1. Wash beans; soak overnight in water to cover.
2. In morning, drain and pick over beans.
3. Place beans in large pot and cover with water until pot is three quarters full.
4. Add ham, onion, celery, bell pepper and parsley. Cook, uncovered, over medium high heat for one hour. Add more water if necessary.
5. Add margarine and cook for additional two hours at lower temperature.
6. Taste for seasoning and add salt and pepper accordingly. Serve hot over rice.

Serves: 4
Preparation: 3½ hours

A very good bean dish. The seasonings are perfect.

Red Beans
Begin night before.

A LA Chez Helene

½	**lb. red beans**
½	**lb. ham shoulder (chunked)**
1	**cup onion (finely chopped)**
1	**stalk celery (finely chopped)**
½	**bell pepper (finely chopped)**
1	**T. parsley**
⅛	**lb. margarine**
	salt and pepper (to taste)

1. Wash beans; soak overnight in water to cover.
2. In morning, drain and pick over beans.
3. Place beans in large pot and cover with water until pot is three quarters full.
4. Add ham, onion, celery, bell pepper and parsley. Cook, uncovered, over medium high heat for one hour. Add more water if necessary.
5. Add margarine and cook for additional two hours at lower temperature.
6. Taste for seasoning and add salt and pepper accordingly. Serve hot over rice.

Serves: 4
Preparation: 3½ hours

A very good bean dish. The seasonings are perfect.

Christian's Restaurant

Christian's Restaurant is noted as much for its location and decor as for its cuisine. Innovative thinking and considerable expenditure have resulted in the renovation and transformation of an old church into one of New Orleans' most unique dining experiences. Located in an uncongested area of the city, with parking available, patrons can wait for seating in the vestibule or have a drink in the tiny bar, formerly the "crying room" for noisy infants. The main dining area utilizes cushioned pews along the walls and various sized tables with captains chairs. The high vaulted ceiling, original overhead beams, amber-glassed cathedral windows and a pervasive use of dark woods, together instill a mood of spaciousness, refinement and calm.

— Continued —

Owner Christian Ansel and Chef Roland Huet have worked to see that the food and its preparation do not take a back seat to decor. "Holiday" awards and inclusion in the "Mobil Guide" and the "Ford Times" attest to these two men's success. The menu features traditional French and Creole cuisines with an emphasis on local seafoods. My dinner consisted of *Oysters Roland* as an appetizer, a fish bisque, mixed green salad, French fried eggplant, *Redfish au Poivre Vert* and a bottle of chilled Chablis. The *Oysters Roland* was not only delicious but was the most creative treatment of this traditional seafood I found while in New Orleans. As to my meal in general, I found no difficulty consuming all that was served me, despite consistently generous portions.

Oysters Roland

A LA Christian's

1	**bunch parsley**
2	**cloves garlic**
1	**12 ounce can mushrooms (drained, reserve juice)**
1	**lb. butter (softened)**
1	**t. black pepper**
1	**t. salt**
¼	**t. nutmeg**
1	**cup bread crumbs**
5	**dozen parboiled oysters**

1. In a blender or food processor, blend in this order: parsley, garlic and mushrooms, until parsley is finely chopped.
2. Add butter and spices and blend again.
3. Add mushroom juice and bread crumbs; blend well.
4. Place six parboiled* oysters in each of four and one half inch au gratin dishes. Smooth butter mixture over them.
5. Place under broiler until brown and bubbly.

Serves: 10 as a first course/5 for entree
Preparation: 20 minutes
Cooking: 10 minutes

Excellent dish for the oyster lover.

* To parboil oysters, place them in a large pot of cold water. Bring water to a boil and cook two-three minutes until oysters are plump. Next, plunge them immediately in cold water to firm them. Drain.

Bouillabaisse

A LA Christian's

⅓	cup olive oil	1½	qts. fish stock
1	onion (finely sliced)	16	shrimp (cooked
3	cloves garlic (chopped)		and peeled)
½	bay leaf	12	oysters
¼	t. thyme	¼	lb. crabmeat
⅛	t. powdered anise	8	fish fillets (cut in
1	tomato (peeled,		small pieces)
	seeded, crushed)	¼	t. saffron
½	cup white wine		

1	long loaf French bread		olive oil
	(¼" thick slices)	2-3	garlic cloves (minced)

— Rouille Sauce —

3	egg yolks	1	t. garlic (minced)
	(room temperature)	¾	t. cayenne pepper
½	qt. olive oil		(or less)

1. Turn burner to medium and heat olive oil in large skillet; add onion slices and saute until transparent.
2. Add garlic, bay leaf, thyme, anise, tomato, wine and fish stock. Simmer uncovered until onions are tender, approximately fifteen to twenty minutes.
3. Add shrimp, oysters, crabmeat and fish fillets. Continue simmering until fish is tender, about ten minutes. Do not overcook fillets.
4. Meanwhile, baste bread with olive oil and sprinkle sparingly with garlic. Toast under broiler until brown.

— Continued —

78

— Rouille Sauce —

5. Beat the egg yolks until thick and sticky, approximately one to two minutes. Continue to beat while adding oil, drop by drop, until sauce thickens and all oil is added. Season with garlic and cayenne pepper.
6. Add saffron to bouillabaise and serve very hot, in large bowls.
7. Let each person garnish bouillabaise to taste with garlic rounds and Rouille sauce.

Serves: 4-6
Preparation: 45 minutes

NOTE: This dish is for garlic lovers. Some palates might enjoy less garlic and cayenne in sauce.

Lobster Madeleine

A LA Christian's

2	T. dry English mustard (ie: Coleman's, etc.)
4	t. water
4	T. butter
3	lbs. lobster meat
⅓	cup brandy
2	cups heavy cream
	salt and pepper (to taste)

1. Mix dry mustard with water to make a light paste. Set aside.
2. In a large pan, melt butter over high heat and saute lobster meat until all water evaporates (about five to seven minutes).
3. Pour brandy over lobster and ignite *. When flame subsides, add cream. Cook and stir until a smooth sauce is obtained.
4. Add mustard paste and blend. Season with salt and pepper and serve in individual casserole dishes or on a platter garnished with parsley.

Serves: 6
Preparation: 20 minutes

* See Glossary of Terms

SINCE 1880
Commander's Palace

Commander's Palace is owned and operated by Ella, Adelaide, Dick and John Brennan. In 1973, having sold their interest in Brennan's restaurant in New Orleans' French Quarter, they took over the personal supervision of "Commander's." It is not uncommon to see them at the reservation desk, in the kitchen or stopping at tables to extend their personal welcome and hospitality to "Commander's" guests.

"Commander's" is located in New Orleans' beautiful Garden District, an area known for elegant old residences and quiet streets. Opened as a restaurant by Emile Commander in 1880, this nineteenth century Victorian home boasts a patio for dining or refreshments and an expansive garden with large cypress, palmetto, ferns, a variety of flowers and strands of moss in all the appropriate places. The interior of "Commander's" can be described as casually elegant with formal dining areas and a festively decorated upstairs dining room where a glass wall allows patrons to enjoy the garden below. The kitchen-bar is a popular area for viewing the restaurant's nerve center without feeling·underfoot.

— Continued —

Executive chef Paul Prudhomme leads a staff that creates such "Commander's" specialties as *Crabmeat Imperial, Trout with Roasted Pecans, Eggs Basin Street* and *Turtle Soup. Veal Lafayette* consists of seasoned white veal sauteed in mushrooms, ham, green onions, then baked. Flamed desserts include *Crepes Kovacs,* mouth watering crepes filled with cream cheese, raisins, liqueur and rum, topped with a rich cream-custard sauce with oranges, spices, pecans and more raisins.

Every Saturday and Sunday the popular "Jazz Brunch" begins at 10:30, featuring New Orleans' jazz greats playing both traditional favorites and requests.

Commander's Garlic Bread

A LA Commander's Palace

1	**loaf French bread (about 14" long)**
¼	**lb. butter**
	garlic powder (to taste)
¼	**cup parsley (finely chopped)**
¼	**cup Parmesan cheese (freshly grated)**

1. Slice bread lengthwise.
2. In a small pan, melt butter; stir in garlic powder.
3. Brush butter/garlic mixture on cut side of bread.
4. Sprinkle with parsley and Parmesan cheese.
5. Cut each half crosswise into one inch pieces.
6. Heat in 425° oven, until hot, about eight minutes, and serve immediately.

Serves: 10
Preparation: 10 minutes

Crab and Corn Bisque

Begin several hours in advance, as stock must cook 3 hours

A LA Commander's Palace

— Stock —

6	medium hard shelled crabs (cleaned)	6	ribs celery (coarsely chopped)
1½	qts. water	2	T. liquid crab broth or bouillon *
2	medium yellow onions (quartered)		

— Bisque —

1½	cups green onions (chopped)		salt (to taste)
			cayenne (to taste)
4	oz. butter	2	(12 oz.) cans corn
2	T. flour		(drained)
	pinch of thyme	1	cup heavy cream
1	t. powdered garlic	1	lb. lump ** crabmeat

— Stock —

1. Place all stock ingredients in a heavy saucepan.
2. Bring to a rolling boil and reduce heat. Simmer for three hours.
3. Strain, reserving crab broth.
4. Measure broth, adding water if necessary to make one quart.

— Continued —

84

— Bisque —

5. In a three quart saucepan, saute onions in butter until soft.
6. Add flour and seasonings; cook until flour begins to stick to pan.
7. Add crab stock and simmer for fifteen minutes.
8. Add corn and simmer fifteen minutes more.
9. Pour in cream; stir well and gently add crab meat.
10. Remove from heat and let stand for thirty minutes.
11. Reheat in a double boiler and stir gently so crabmeat does not break up and cream does not curdle.

Serves: 8
Preparation: 1 hour
Cooking: 3 hours
Set time: ½ hour
Total: 4½ hours

*You may purchase the bouillon in gourmet section of grocery or you may use the liquid from canned crab.
**See Glossary of Terms.

Praline Parfait

A LA Commander's Palace

— Praline Sauce —

1½   cups white Karo syrup
1½   cups dark Karo syrup
1½   cups chopped pecans
1   t. vanilla
     dash nutmeg
     dash cinnamon

12   scoops vanilla ice cream
1   cup cream (whipped)
6   maraschino cherries

— Praline Sauce —

1.   Mix first six ingredients together to make the sauce.

2.   For each serving, place a little praline sauce in dish. Top with two scoops of ice cream and a generous amount of praline sauce over top.
3.   Garnish with whipped cream and cherry.

Serves: 6
Preparation: 15 minutes

A deliciously simple dessert, guaranteed to please any sweet tooth! My family's favorite!

The Embers
Steak House, Inc.

One of New Orleans' best establishments for quality steaks and beef is The Embers Steak House. Located in the French Quarter since 1957, The Embers Steak House serves six different cuts of char-broiled steaks, broiled lamb chops and for any lost seafarers, there is the broiled filet of trout. To accompany the above entrees there is the special baked potato stuffed with sour cream, cheese and chives, a tossed green salad with a choice of two homemade dressings and hot French rolls.

The decor of The Embers Steak House is worth noting. The dining area features subdued lighting, natural brick, rough hewn rafters and a large fireplace bolstering an assortment of copperware. The fact that the steaks are cooked within view of both diners and sidewalk pedestrians only serves to whet the appetites of each as flames lick the undersides of lean rib eyes, T-bones and filet mignons.

For prior or post dining relaxation, a second floor balcony overlooks the intersection of Bourbon and St. Peter streets. This is an excellent location from which to enjoy an Irish coffee and gaze down upon youngsters doing a soft-shoe to the highly audible sounds issuing from several nearby jazz halls.

— Continued —

Starting in the restaurant business at fourteen years of age as a dishwasher, Embers' owner Roger McConnell and his uncle later opened the original Embers at a different location in the French Quarter before moving to their present address at 700 Bourbon Street. Mr. McConnell has also served as president of the Louisiana Restaurant Association and the New Orleans Food Festival.

Dressing (French type)
(Age for two weeks before serving)

A LA - The Embers Steak House

1	small onion (chopped)
1	clove garlic (minced)
2½	T. tomato soup
2½	T. water
1½	t. sugar
½	cup salad oil
¼	cup vinegar
6	T. chili sauce
½	t. dry mustard
½	t. pepper
1	t. salt
1½	t. Worchestershire sauce
	pinch of celery seed
2	drops Tabasco sauce

1. Combine all ingredients in a large jar and shake well. Refrigerate.
2. Allow to age for two weeks before serving.

Makes: 1 pint
Preparation: 15 minutes

Excellent!

Roquefort Cheese Dressing

A LA - The Embers Steak House

10   **oz. imported Roquefort cheese**
12   **oz. cream cheese**
2   **T. mayonnaise**
½   **cup white vinegar**
½   **cup salad oil**
2   **T. sugar**
1½   **t. salt**
1   **t. pepper**

1.   Blend all ingredients with electric mixer until smooth and fluffy.
2.   Refrigerate.

Yield: 1 pint
Preparation: 10 minutes

A must for Roquefort dressing lovers!

Special Stuffed Potato

A LA - The Embers Steak House

Idaho baking potatoes (1 large–12 oz. per person)

For each potato you will need:

2	**t. butter**
	salt and pepper (to taste)
4	**t. sour cream**
1	**t. chopped chives (frozen or dry)**
3	**t. sharp cheese * (coarsely grated)**

1. Bake potato(es) at 450° for one hour or until done.
2. Make lengthwise slit in each potato, three to four inches long.
3. Carefully insert fork into slit and break potato away from skin, so that potato is left inside skin but is broken up. While doing this, add butter, salt and pepper.
4. Add sour cream, chives and grated cheese. Mix into potato being careful not to break skin.
5. Sprinkle each potato with additional cheese. Bake for seven minutes or until cheese melts and begins to brown at edges.

Yield: 1 large potato per person
Preparation: 30 minutes
Baking: 1 hour 10 minutes

* The Ember's recommends using Wisconsin Black Rind Midget Cheese.

Bourbon Street

Galatoire's

Since opening in 1905, Galatoire's is one of the few establishments on Bourbon Street to endure. Once the address of stately residences, titled peoples and cultural events, Bourbon Street now boasts strip joints, peepshows and tee shirt shops whose stenciled inventories would bring a rush of crimson to the likes of Mae West. Galatoire's still flourishes because of its quality food and attentive service.

Founded by Jean Galatoire, the restaurant was largely developed into its present image under the leadership of Jean's nephew, Justin Galatoire. Currently the restaurant is ably managed by a third generation family member, Yvonne Galatoire Wynne and three, fourth generation family members–David Gooch, Leon Galatoire and Justin Galatoire Frey.

The food is bought fresh daily in amounts designed to avoid leftovers. Although the menu has no pitfalls, seafoods have been the cornerstone upon which Galatoire's rests. *Shrimp Remoulade, Crabmeat Yvonne, Trout Meuniere Almondine* and *Trout Marguery* are some of Galatoire's great dishes. Chef Charles Plough has expertly guided the preparation of foods at Galatoire's since 1952.

— Continued —

The equal treatment of patrons and attentive service are traditions developed during the era of Justin Galatoire. To avoid showing favoritism, reservations are never taken and the line forms to the rear for one of the forty tables and seventeen waiters.

Crabmeat Yvonne

A LA Galatoire's

2	T. butter
1	medium size can sliced mushrooms
6	fresh artichoke bottoms (cooked and sliced)
2	lbs. lump crabmeat *
	salt and pepper (to taste)
6	lemon slices
	parsley (chopped for garnish)

1. In a medium skillet, saute mushrooms in butter over low heat until warm. (Do not brown butter).
2. Add artichoke slices and saute gently, keeping artichokes firm.
3. Fold in crabmeat and salt and pepper. Cook one to two minutes.
4. Serve immediately, garnished with lemon slice and parsley.

Serves: 6
Preparation: 20 minutes

Delicious and so easy to do!

* See Glossary of Terms

Shrimp Remoulade

Appetizer (start several hours in advance)

A LA Galatoire's

1	bunch green onions		salt and pepper
1	stalk celery	⅓	cup wine vinegar
2	cloves garlic	⅔	cup olive oil
1	sprig fresh parsley	2½	lbs. large
5	T. creole mustard*		green ** shrimp
2	T. paprika		

1. Grind all vegetables together until very fine.
2. Add to the vegetables: mustard, paprika, salt and pepper.
3. Add vinegar and mix thoroughly. Gradually add olive oil.
4. Let mixture stand a few hours.
5. Drop shrimp in boiling water for about three to four minutes. Never overcook. Afterwards, shell and devein shrimp. Next, soak shrimp in marinade in refrigerator for three hours.
6. Remove shrimp from marinade and arrange on a bed of shredded lettuce and serve very cold.

Serves: 6
Preparation: 20 minutes
Marinade: 3 hours/3 hours

* You may use Poupon Mustard.
** Green shrimp refers to shrimp in their shells.

Trout Meuniere Almondine

═══════════════════════════════

A LA Galatoire's

6	**medium trout filets (skinned)**
	flour
	salt
	pepper
¼	**lb. butter**
1	**lemon (juiced)**
	parsley (chopped)
½	**cup sliced almonds (roasted) ***

1. Sprinkle trout filets with flour and season with salt and pepper.
2. Melt butter in frying pan; add fish and cook very slowly until brown on both sides.
3. Remove fish to a warm platter and keep warm.
4. To butter remaining in pan, add lemon juice and a little chopped parsley.
5. Pour this brown butter over the filets. Garnish with roasted almonds and serve.

Preparation: 10 minutes
Cooking: 15-20 minutes
Serves: 4-6

Delicious dish!!

* If you like, you can roast your own almonds in oven at 400° for about five minutes.

Patissier at LaMarquise

LA MARQUISE

French Pastry Shop

La Marquise, a small French pastry shop hidden among the numerous other small shops in the French Quarter, belongs somewhere other than in a world of inflation, suffering and sorrow. It should be nestled in a sugar-spun world of eternal youth, smiling faces and a gentle sun.

Propietor and patissier, Maurice Delechelle, a young man of modest proportions, is a white-clad Santa to the city's sweet-toothed. He's the village Pied Piper, whose innocently adorned windows lure unsuspecting sugar-seekers of all ages. These windows, that showcase delicate paper doves whose beaks carry the lightest of pastries and a carousel whose agreeable steed bears a saddle full of creamy delights, lie but a few feet from the well-worn doorknob.

Once inside, tables and chairs stand between the onlooker and a pastry counter whose selection of fifty different creations reflect the accomplishments of a man who began baking in his native France in 1957 and has since refined his talents from Nice to Guadeloupe.

— Continued —

There are *Strawberry Napoleons, Croissants* that are sold at the rate of over three thousand per week, *Swan-Shaped Cream Puffs, Tartes Milanaise* with their magnificent fresh fruit designs over a custard layer, *Butter Cream Squares, Rum Balls, Quiche Lorraine* and a most remarkable *Cheese Cake.* To accompany the above, La Marquise serves coffee, tea, lemonade and homemade chocolate – made with whole milk.

Purchases can be savored inside or on the outdoor patio screened from the street and adjoining buildings by a high stone wall and assorted broad-leafed trees that house a variety of song birds.

Caramel Custard

A LA - La Marquise

1	**quart milk**
1	**cup (plus 2 T.) granulated sugar**
6	**whole eggs**
2	**yolks**
1	**t. vanilla**
10	**(8 oz.) custard cups**

1. Boil milk and remove from stove.
2. Cook sugar in a saucepan until light brown in color. Pour sugar into milk.
3. Beat eggs and yolks together with vanilla. Pour a little of milk-sugar mixture into eggs; mix well and pour back into saucepan with milk and sugar and mix.
4. Fill ten custard cups with custard mix. Set cups in a pan with cold water and bake in 300° oven for approximately forty five minutes. Don't let water boil.
5. Serve cold.

Serves: 10
Cooking/Baking: 10 minutes/45 minutes (includes preparation)

A tasty, light dessert!

Quiche Lorraine

A LA - La Marquise

— Pie shell —

2	cups flour	1	t. salt
¼	cup Crisco	¼	cup cold water

— Filling —

¼	lb. ham (cubed)	½	t. salt
¼	lb. bacon (cubed)		pinch pepper
2	cups whipping cream		pinch nutmeg
2	eggs (beaten)	¼	lb. Swiss cheese (cubed)

— Pie shell —

1. Preheat oven to 400°.
2. Cut shortening into flour; add salt. Add water and stir until dough forms a ball.
3. Roll out pie shell and line a 9" or 10" pie pan. Precook pie shell for eight minutes. Set aside.
4. Lower oven temperature to 325°.

— Filling —

5. Saute ham and bacon over medium heat. Drain.
6. Combine whipping cream, eggs, salt, pepper and nutmeg in a bowl and beat together.
7. Sprinkle ham, bacon and cheese on bottom of pie shell. Pour over whipping cream mixture.
8. Bake at 325° for fifty to sixty minutes.

Serves: 4-6
Preparation: 45 minutes
Baking: 50-60 minutes

A good rendition of this classic dish!

Marti's attracts a broad spectrum of New Orleans' citizenry including artists and patrons of the arts. Located across from the Cultural Center, Marti's beckons aficionados of the stage, screen and string sections as well as writers, actors and actresses. However, the path to Marti's door is not culturally exclusive. Any devotee of fine culinary productions and pleasant scenery is welcome to tread and many do.

Marti's own contribution to the arts is Chef Henry Robertson. His kitchen is his garret and his organic renderings reflect over thirty years experience. The fact that Chef Robertson is also an ordained minister may explain his devotion to his duties. The ingredients and preparation are consistently high quality and

— Continued —

his accomplishments range from appetizers to desserts. Specifically, the *Corn and Shrimp Chowder* is often called for an encore and the *Eggplant Stuffed with Shrimp and Crabmeat* can cling to one's memory. The casseroles, the omelettes and *Spinach Salad* all deserve sustained applause. The desserts pose a dilemma. Does one order the *Strawberry Ice*, the touted *Bread Pudding* or the *Praline Sundae* – which is often contested for between staff and customer. For those who forgot their opera glasses or just dislike reading menus, a large blackboard lists the daily specials which can include such magnum opuses as *Roast Duckling with Fig Glaze*, *Capon* or a *Crab and Oyster Casserole*.

Marti's decor is neither French Cafe, Old New Orleans nor Louis XIV. Marti's could more appropriately be described as chic, stylish and Upper Manhattan. A compromising elegance gives equal billing to denim or cummerbund.

Gazpacho Soup

A LA - La Marti's

3	ripe tomatoes (peeled and quartered)
⅓	cup white onion (chopped)
½	cup green pepper (chopped)
¼	cup cucumber (seeded and chopped)
2	t. salt
1	clove garlic
¼	t. white pepper
⅛	t. Tabasco
1	t. Worcestershire sauce
2	T. olive oil
2	T. lemon juice
¾	cup tomato juice

1. Place all ingredients in blender and puree.
2. Press through sieve to remove seeds.
3. Serve chilled.

Serves: 6
Preparation: 10 minutes
Refrigeration: (varies depending on temperature of ingredients)

═══════════════════════════

A LA - La Marti's

4½ **cups chicken stock**
2 **cups long grain white rice**
3 **T. flour**
½ **cup oil**
1 **cup onions (finely chopped)**
1½ **lbs. chicken livers (finely chopped)**
½ **cup celery (chopped)**
½ **cup parsley (finely chopped)**
1 **cup green onions (chopped)**
½ **cup green pepper (finely chopped)**
1 **t. garlic (minced)**
   salt (to taste)
   pepper (to taste)
⅛ **t. cayenne pepper**

1. In a large pan bring four cups of stock to boil (reserve one half cup stock); add rice and cover. Cook rice until fluffy, approximately twenty five minutes.
2. Meanwhile, brown flour in large pan over medium heat; add oil to make a roux.*
3. Add onions and cook until brown.
4. Stir in chicken livers, celery, parsley, green onions, green pepper, and garlic. Cook for five minutes.
5. Pour in one half cup stock and cook fifteen minutes more.
6. Remove from heat; skim any excess fat from top of mixture.
7. Fold in rice and correct seasonings.*
8. Serve immediately, or if served later, warm in 350° oven for twenty minutes.

— Continued —

Serves: 6 generously (may be served as entree or side dish)
Preparation: 45 minutes

For chicken liver lovers, a great dish!

* See Glossary of Terms

Crab or Shrimp Mornay

A LA - La Marti's

8	fresh artichokes	¼	t. cayenne
½	cup butter	2½	oz. imported
½	cup flour		Swiss cheese
¼	cup onion (grated)	2	T. lemon juice
½	cup green onion (chopped)	2	lbs. lump crabmeat* OR 3 lbs. shrimp (boiled & peeled)
2	T. parsley (chopped)		
2	cups heavy cream	½	lb. fresh mushrooms (thickly sliced)
1	cup dry white wine		
2½	t. salt	3	T. Romano cheese
½	t. white pepper		

1. Boil artichokes until tender; scrape leaves (reserving pulp) and quarter bottoms. Set aside.
2. In a two quart saucepan melt butter; stir in flour and cook five minutes over medium heat, stirring constantly.
3. Add onion and green onion. Saute two to three minutes; do not brown.
4. Stir in parsley; gradually add cream and simmer until hot.
5. Add wine, salt, white pepper, cayenne. Blend well and simmer, stirring occasionally.
6. Add Swiss cheese and stir. Cover; turn off heat and allow to cool.
7. When sauce is cool, stir in lemon juice and scrapings from artichoke leaves.
8. In a three quart casserole, alternate layers of crabmeat, quartered artichoke bottoms and sliced raw mushrooms, using sauce between layers and on top.
9. Sprinkle Romano cheese on top. Cover and refrigerate until ready to use.**
10. To warm, place room temperature casserole into 350° oven, heat thirty to forty-five minutes. If top does not brown, place under broiler for three to five minutes.

— Continued —

Serves: 8
Cooking/Baking: 30/45 minutes
Preparation: 35 minutes

Comments: Excellent! Better if made ahead. It is very rich, needs only a green salad & French bread served with it.

* See Glossary of Terms
** You can make this dish in the morning and refrigerate until baking time. This makes for a hassle free dinner party.

Cream of Artichoke Soup

(Can be served hot or cold. Begin several hours ahead)

A LA - La Marti's

4	large or 6 medium artichokes	¼	cup lemon juice
6	T. butter	1	bay leaf
½	cup onions (finely chopped)	1	t. salt
		¼	t. pepper
½	cup celery (finely chopped)	¼	t. thyme
		2	egg yolks (beaten)
6	T. flour	2	cups light cream
6	cups clear chicken stock		lemon slices (garnish) chopped parsley (garnish)

1. Boil artichokes in water until done, approximately one hour. Drain. Scrape pulp from leaves. Discard leaves and reserve pulp. Remove fibrous choke; finely chop bottoms and set aside.
2. In large saucepan, saute onion and celery in butter until soft but not brown. Add flour; cook one minute, stirring constantly. Stir in stock and lemon juice until well blended.
3. Season with bay leaf, salt, pepper and thyme; add artichoke bottoms and pulp scrapings. Cover and simmer twenty minutes until slightly thickened.
4. Puree soup in blender for a smooth, creamy consistency.
5. Beat yolks and cream together; set aside.
6. Heat soup to boiling point; remove from heat; add cream and egg mixture. Correct seasonings.
7. If served cold, chill thoroughly.
8. Keep warm over hot water, if soup will be served hot.
9. Garnish with thin lemon slices topped with parsley and serve.

— Continued —

Cream of Artichoke Soup — Continued

Serves: 6-8
Preparation: 2 hours
(If served chilled, allow a couple of hours refrigeration time).

A delicious summer or winter soup!

Filet de Boeuf aux Champignons
(Begin 3-4 hours before serving time)

A LA - La Marti's

3-5	lbs. tenderloin of beef	1	carrot (sliced)
2	T. olive oil	1	T. onion (chopped)
1	T. salt	4	T. lemon juice
¼	t. cayenne pepper freshly ground black pepper (to taste)	3	cups beef stock or bouillon

— Sauce —

6	T. butter (divided)	½	cup Madeira wine
3	T. flour (browned)*	2	cups small mushrooms
2	cups stock (reserved from beef)	1½	dozen sliced truffles (optional)

1. Rub tenderloin with oil, salt and peppers. Place in pan on top of carrots and onions; pour on lemon juice and let stand for two to three hours.
2. Preheat oven to 500°.
3. Pour stock over meat and bake for five minutes. Reduce oven to 350° and cook to desired doneness, approximately forty minutes for rare.
4. Remove and place on heated serving platter and keep warm. Reserve two cups stock.

— Sauce —

5. Melt two tablespoons butter and add browned flour, stirring until smooth. Add reserved stock and Madeira, stirring slowly to thicken. Cook for fifteen minutes over medium heat.

— Continued —

6. In separate pan saute mushrooms (and truffles) in remaining butter and add to sauce.
7. To serve: slice meat and arrange. Serve warmed sauce in heated gravy boat.

Serves: 4-6
Preparation: 35 minutes
Baking: 40 minutes for rare

An elegant beef dish that won raves at my house.
Serving idea: Accompany with Marti's Garlic Grits.

* See Glossary of Terms

A LA - La Marti's

2	lbs. beef round steak (½" thick)	1	cup tomatoes (chopped)
¼	cup bacon grease	¼	t. tarragon (optional)
¼	cup flour	¼	t. thyme
½	cup onion (chopped)	½	cup water
1	cup green onions (chopped)	½	cup red wine
		1½	t. salt
¼	cup celery (chopped)	¼	t. black pepper
¾	cup green pepper (chopped)	1	bay leaf
		¼	t. Tabasco
1	clove garlic (minced)	1	T. Worcestershire sauce
		1½	t. parsley (chopped)

1. Cut meat into serving size pieces. Remove fat and pound to one quarter inch thick.
2. Melt two tablespoons bacon grease in dutch oven; brown meat well; remove to warm plate.
3. Add remaining grease and flour to dutch oven. Cook, stirring constantly until flour is well blended and dark brown.
4. Add onion, green onions, celery, green pepper and garlic. Saute until limp. Add tomatoes, tarragon and thyme and cook for three minutes.
5. Stir in water and wine, mixing well with vegetables and spices.
6. Return meat to dutch oven. Season with salt, pepper, bay leaf, Tabasco, Worcestershire and parsley. Turn heat to low and cook for two hours until very tender. More liquid can be added to prevent drying out.
7. Serve warm over rice or grits.

— Continued —

Grillades — Continued

━━━━━━━━━━━━━━━━━━━━━━━━━━━━━━━━━━━

Serves: 4
Preparation: 45 minutes
Cooking: 2 hours

NOTE: Grillades can be made in advance, kept in refrigerator and heated thoroughly just before serving.

A delicious, hearty dish!

Garlic Grits

(Begin several hours ahead)

A LA - La Marti's

1	cup grits
1	qt. water
1½	t. salt
½	cup Cheddar cheese (grated)
1-2	cloves garlic (pressed, discard hull)
¼	cup butter
2	eggs (slightly beaten)
1	cup milk
2	T. Parmesan cheese (grated)

1. Cook grits in boiling salted water until tender, but still pourable, about five minutes.
2. Remove from heat, add Cheddar cheese, garlic and butter, stirring until melted. Allow to cool about thirty minutes.
3. Preheat oven to 325°.
4. Add eggs and milk to grits mixture; pour into greased two quart casserole.
5. Bake for fifty - sixty minutes; remove from oven; sprinkle with Parmesan cheese and bake for ten minutes more. Serve immediately.

Serves: 4-6
Preparation: 15 minutes
Baking: 70 minutes

Delicious accompaniment to Marti's Filet de Boeuf or any roast meat. May be prepared ahead and baked before serving.

Masson's
Restaurant Français

Masson's well kept, white clad building and ample parking area reside along the shore of Lake Pontchartrain, far from downtown New Orleans and the French Quarter.

Upon entering Masson's, I found the foyer walls supporting such honors as eleven "Holiday" awards, four "Mobil Four Star" awards, citations from the "Guild of Sommeliers" and "Campagnon de Bordeaux" for excellence in wines, an honorary "Master of Wines" degree from Loyola University and letters of appreciation from past diners including, then President of the United States, Gerald Ford.

Albert and Ernest Masson, continuing in their parents' and grandparents' footsteps, have assembled a talented staff that carries out its duties with skill and regard for the patron. Chef Robert Finley directs the preparation of award-winning meals in a clean, orderly kitchen and oversees the development of several aspiring chefs, including Albert, Jr., as part of the restaurant's participation in the American Culinary Federation's Junior Chefs Apprenticeship Program.

— Continued —

Masson's profiles its cuisine as French Provincial with a Creole influence only in its seasonings. Classifications aside, time and distance have not diminished pleasant thoughts of my dinner there which included *Crabmeat and Artichoke* as the hors d'oeuvre, *Duckling Roti Orange Cherry Sauce*, a *Baked Banana in Brandy Sauce* and the *Almond Torte*.

Reservations are essential.

Crabmeat and Artichoke

A LA Masson's Restaurant Francais

¼	lb. margarine or butter
¼	cup green onions (thinly sliced)
2	bay leaves
	pinch of cayenne pepper
	pinch of thyme
¼	cup white wine
1	lb. lump crabmeat
1	egg (beaten)
½	cup fine bread crumbs
6	artichoke bottoms
1	cup Swiss cheese (grated)
1½	cups Hollandaise sauce *

Preheat oven to 350°.

1. Saute green onions, bay leaves, cayenne pepper and thyme in melted butter for three minutes.
2. Add wine and crabmeat; fold in egg and breadcrumbs. Mold into six balls.
3. Place artichoke bottoms in buttered ovenproof dish; top with crabmeat mixture.
4. Sprinkle with grated cheese and bake in oven for ten minutes.
5. Top with Hollandaise sauce and serve immediately.

Serves: 6
Preparation: 15 minutes
Baking: 10 minutes

A very easy and elegant first course or luncheon dish.

* See recipe p. 3. Also see *A La San Francisco / Restaurant Recipes* book p. 64, or use your favorite recipe.

Les Merveilles de la Mer en Crepes

Seafood Crepes

━━━━━━━━━━━━━━━━━━━━━━━━━━━━━━━━

A LA Masson's Restaurant Francais

8	thin crepes (see LeRuth's recipe p. 154 or use your favorite recipe)	1	pt. light cream
		3-4	large egg yolks (beaten)
		½	lb. lobster meat (cooked)
½	lb. butter (divided)		
½	cup green onions (chopped)	½	lb. shrimp pieces (cooked)
½	cup mushrooms (sliced)	½	lb crabmeat (cooked)
3	t. flour	2	t. cognac
½	cup white wine		

1. Make crepes and set aside.
2. Melt one cube butter in pan and saute green onions and mushrooms. Add flour and cook two - three minutes, stirring constantly.
3. Add wine and cream and simmer eight - ten minutes.
4. Remove from heat and stir in enough egg yolks to make a medium sauce. Set aside.
5. Melt remaining cube of butter in another pan and saute all seafood four - five minutes.
6. Add cognac and ignite*. When flame dies, divide sauce and add half to seafood. Mix well.
7. Spread each crepe with one eighth of mixture and roll up.
8. Pour remaining sauce over crepes and serve.

Serves: 4
Preparation: 45 minutes (does not include crepe preparation time)

A great seafood dish! Equally good over rice or noodles.

* See "Flambe" in Glossary of Terms.

Oyster and Artichoke Soup

A LA Masson's Restaurant Francais

⅔   stick butter
1   bunch green onions (chopped)
    pinch of thyme
    pinch of cayenne
3   bay leaves
2   T. flour
1   can (14 oz.) chicken broth
1   pint extra oyster water *
1   pint oysters (small)
1   can (14 oz.) artichoke hearts (chopped)
3   sprigs parsley (chopped)
    salt (to taste)
½   cup whipping cream

1. In a large skillet, melt butter and saute onions, thyme, cayenne and bay leaves.
2. Add flour and stir well with wire whip until smooth.
3. Slowly add chicken broth and oyster water, stirring constantly to blend.
4. Simmer for fifteen minutes.
5. Add oysters (with their own water if canned), chopped artichoke hearts, and parsley. Simmer an additional ten minutes. Salt to taste.
6. Stir in whipping cream just before serving.

Serves: 6
Preparation: 45 minutes

Great flavor – a hearty seafood soup.

* Ask for this at your butcher or seafood house or buy canned in grocery store.

Sabayon

A sweet custard dessert
(Begin several hours in advance)

A LA Masson's Restaurant Francais

6	**eggs (separated)**
¾	**cup sugar**
¾	**cup cream sherry**
¾	**cup heavy cream (whipped)**
1	**t. vanilla**

1. Beat egg yolks with sugar until creamy.
2. Add sherry and cook in a double boiler until thick, stirring occasionally.
3. Pour into bowl and cool ten to fifteen minutes.
4. Fold in whipped cream; add vanilla.
5. Fold in stiffly beaten egg whites.
6. Divide into six small ramekins or custard cups; chill two to three hours.

Serves: 6
Preparation: 40 minutes
Refrigeration: 2-3 hours

Comments: Very rich! Small portions are just right.

Supreme of Trout with Crabmeat Sauce

A LA Masson's Restaurant Francais

4	filets of trout (6-8 oz. each) salt (to taste) pepper (to taste)	½	cup dry white wine
2	lemons	2	cups heavy cream salt (to taste) pepper (to taste)
½	cup butter	2-3	egg yolks (beaten)
½	cup green onions (chopped)	1½	lbs. crabmeat (cooked)

1. Season filets with salt and pepper. Place in broiling pan.
2. Squeeze juice from one half lemon over each filet. Set aside until ready to broil.
3. In a medium sized skillet, melt butter and saute onions until soft. Add wine and cream; stir.
4. Simmer five to eight minutes; salt and pepper to taste.
5. Broil filets until tender.
6. While filets are broiling, remove sauce from heat; stir in beaten egg yolks and fold in crabmeat.
7. Place cooked filets on a serving dish and cover with crab-meat sauce.

Serves: 4
Preparation: 10 minutes
Total cooking time: 20 minutes

Fabulous!! Looks terrific served over a bed of rice.

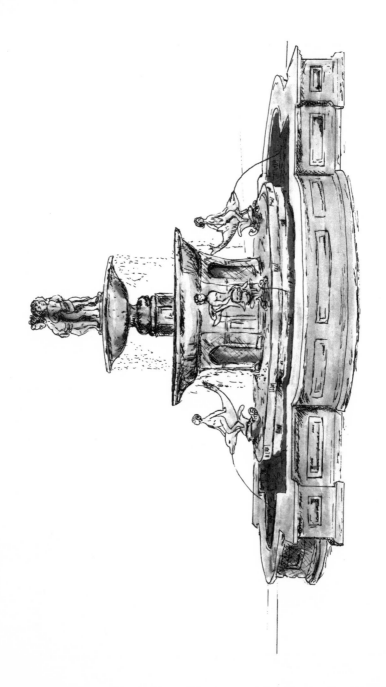

Fountain of the Arts

La Provence

The German poet Johann Goethe said, "A man does not learn to understand anything unless he loves it." Chef Chris Kerageorgiou, owner and operator of La Provence, exemplifies this timeless observation. Chris's daily "Labor of Love" has produced growing ranks of loyal patrons, the "Holiday" award and charitable dinners for elderly and handicapped since La Provence opened in the autumn of 1972.

Chef Chris, a native of Port Saint Louis, France, describes his cuisine as very French with constant attention paid to simplicity in preparation and presentation. The homemade pates and sausages are popular among those with light appetites and go well with French bread and a bottle of wine from the well-stocked cellar. Entree items include current European dishes and original recipes. Fish, shellfish, beef and fowl all grace the menu. *Le Poisson Rouge Alfonso* is a sauteed redfish, stuffed with crabmeat, mushrooms and topped with bearnaise sauce. The *Peppercorn Steak* is characteristic of French cooking's simplicity and offers a novel means of preparation. *Le Canard au Poivre Vert* offers sections of roast duck in a sauce consisting of cognac, white wine, crushed Madagascar peppercorns, shallots and butter. Desserts include homemade ice creams, cheesecake and baklava.

— Continued —

A trip to La Provence provides the diner with more than just cuisine. Located on the northern shore of Lake Pontchartrain, this rustic country-inn lies enshrined amidst forests of lofty pine, clean air and natural reservoirs of delicious spring water. Once seated, the efficacy of the dining room staff allows you to further enjoy the comfort and tasteful decor of the dining area and the sylvan view through windows that invite a touch to confirm their presence.

Salad Dressing

A LA - La Provence

1	oz. garlic
3	oz. anchovies
3	oz. prepared mustard
4	eggs (beaten)
2	T. oregano
½	cup wine vinegar
½	cup lemon juice
	salt and pepper (to taste)
4	cups salad oil

1. Blend together garlic and anchovies in a blender.
2. Add mustard, eggs and oregano. Mix well.
3. Add the wine vinegar, lemon juice and salt and pepper.
4. Slowly add the salad oil, until well combined.

Yield: 6 cups
Preparation: 20 minutes

A most unusual flavor. Delicious!

Poulet Fromage
Chicken with Creamy Cheese Sauce

A LA - La Provence

1   2 or 3 lb. fryer (cut in pieces)
½   cup butter
2   t. shallots (chopped)
½   cup dry vermouth
¾   cup heavy cream
     salt and pepper
     piece of waxed paper *(lightly covered with oil)*
2   T. grated Swiss cheese
1   T. blue cheese (softened)
1   T. butter (softened)
1   t. Dijon mustard

1.   Preheat oven to 350°. Melt butter in pan (use a skillet or pan that can be put in oven) and saute chicken (be careful not to brown). Add shallots and vermouth and reduce* liquid slightly.
2.   Add enough cream to almost cover chicken; season with salt and pepper. Bring to a boil then remove from heat and cover dish with oiled waxed paper.
3.   Bake in oven for fifteen to twenty minutes.
4.   Remove from oven; transfer chicken to heated platter and keep warm.
5.   Strain sauce by passing it through fine strainer. Return to a clean pan and reduce* over medium heat.
6.   Whip Swiss cheese, blue cheese, butter and mustard into cream sauce. Pour over chicken and serve.

— Continued —

Poulet Fromage — Continued

Serves: 3-4
Preparation: 30 minutes
Baking: 15-20 minutes

A nice change of pace for chicken. Flavors blend nicely!

* See Glossary of Terms

═══════════════════════════════
═══════════════════════════════

A LA - La Provence

Crepes (Use LeRuth's recipe for "Crepes a la Ritz" p. 154 or use a favorite recipe)

— Cream Sauce — * (yields 2 cups)

¼	**cup flour**
4	**T. butter (melted)**
2	**cups milk**
2	**T. chopped shallots**
1	**bay leaf**
	pinch of nutmeg
	salt and pepper (to taste)

1	**lb. country ham, diced** *(or substitute a quality dry cured)*
¼	**cup butter**
2	**cups fresh mushrooms (chopped)**
½	**cup green onions (chopped)**
1	**cup dry sherry**
2	**bay leaves**
¼	**cup tomatoes (diced)**
¾	**cup Swiss cheese (grated)**

1. Prepare crepes and set aside.

— Cream Sauce —

2. In a small saucepan, stir flour into melted butter to make a roux**. Slowly add milk and stir with wire whisk until smooth.
3. Add shallots, bay leaf, nutmeg and seasonings. Cook over very low heat, stirring constantly for about fifteen minutes. Strain. Set aside and keep warm.

— Continued —

4. Blanch ham in boiling water for ten minutes. Drain.
5. Meanwhile, melt butter and saute mushrooms and onions together until dry, about ten minutes.
6. Combine mushrooms, ham and sherry. Simmer with bay leaves until most of liquid is gone. Add tomatoes.
7. Measure out half the cream sauce (one cup) and one half cup of the grated cheese and add to ham-mushroom mixture. Stir.
8. In a separate pan, combine remaining cream sauce and grated cheese to make a Mornay Sauce. Stir this over low heat until cheese has melted and sauce is hot.
9. Spread each crepe with ham mixture; roll and top with Mornay Sauce. Serve immediately.

Serves: 4
Preparation: 30 minutes (add twenty minutes (approx.) for crepe preparation)

Delicious crepe filling–probably equally good over white rice!

* This cream sauce comes from our own test kitchen. You may substitute your favorite recipe if you like.
** See Glossary of Terms.

Coq au Vin
Chicken with Wine Sauce

A LA - La Provence

2½ **- 3½ lb. frying chicken (cut up)**
¼ **cup butter**
2 **cups red wine (or more)**
¼ **cup shallots (chopped)**
½ **t. black pepper**
½ **t. thyme**
2 **bay leaves**
2 **T. butter**
1 **cup pearl onions (cooked)**
1 **cup sliced, fresh mushrooms (sauteed)**

1. Preheat oven to 375°.
2. In a large skillet, melt butter and slowly saute chicken. (Do not brown).
3. Add red wine to cover. Add shallots, pepper, thyme and bay leaves. Cover pan and bake at 375° for forty minutes.
4. When chicken is done, remove to serving dish and keep warm. Put pan with wine juices on top of burner.
5. On medium heat, reduce* liquid to one and one half cups. Whip in butter to make a rich sauce.
6. Pour sauce over chicken and garnish dish with pearl onions and mushrooms.

Serves: 4
Preparation: 15 minutes
Baking: 40 minutes

* See Glossary of Terms

Pepper Steak

A LA - La Provence

4	prime steak filets (8 oz. each)
½	cup butter
1	T. green peppercorns*
2	T. shallots (finely chopped)
¼	cup brandy
1	pt. heavy cream
2	T. lemon juice
	salt and pepper

1. Make sauce by melting butter and sauteing green peppercorns and shallots. Add brandy and flambe**. Add cream, lemon juice, salt and pepper. Reduce** liquid until it makes a thick sauce, stirring continually.
2. Meanwhile, cook steaks as desired.
3. Pour sauce over steaks and serve.

Serves: 4
Cooking: 25 minutes (includes preparation)

Delicious if you like green peppercorns.

* Green peppercorns may be purchased at gourmet food shops and specialty stores.
** See Glossary of Terms.

Baked Oysters John Batiste Reboul

A LA - La Provence

3	**lbs. fresh mushrooms (chopped)**
¼	**cup butter**
4	**oz. garlic (finely chopped)**
2	**oz. shallots or white part of green onion (finely chopped)**
3	**cups dry white wine**
1-2	**bay leaves**
	pinch of thyme
	salt and pepper (to taste)
1-1½	**lbs. small fresh oysters**
1	**cup Hollandaise sauce** (use favorite recipe or packaged sauce)

1. Preheat oven to 450°.
2. In a small skillet melt butter and saute mushrooms; add garlic and shallots. Cook until limp.
3. Add white wine, bay leaves, thyme, salt and pepper. Reduce* liquid in half by cooking to a sauce-like consistency.
4. Place oysters in casserole dish and cover with mushroom sauce.
5. Cook in oven for twenty five minutes until done.
6. Cover with Hollandaise sauce and place under broiler to brown.

Serves: 4
Preparation: 35 minutes
Baking: 25 minutes

Rich flavor

* See Glossary of Terms

LA RIVIERA

With the preponderance of Creole and Cajun cooking in and around New Orleans, people whose palates hoist different flags on different days might ask – "Where does one find a good ethnic restaurant?"

Located in Metairie, twenty minutes by car from the streets of The Great Gumbo, remoulade sauce and bread pudding, there resides the Italian port of La Riviera. The major-domo and head chef is Goffredo Fraccaro, a native of Tortona, Italy. Before arriving in the United States in 1961, Goffredo served his apprenticeship in Italy, Germany, England and as chief steward aboard the great Italian luxury ships. Resembling a seasoned Pillsbury Doughboy, Goffredo's curly, white hair, florid cheeks and ebullient disposition is in keeping with sun-filled skies, pastas laden with rich, red sauces and full-bodied wines.

— Continued —

135

La Riviera draws most of its customers from local loyalists. The specialty is veal. Over a thousand pounds of this tender meat is sold weekly as the basic ingredient for seven different dishes, all cooked to order. The pasta is homemade and includes *Tortellini, Canneloni, Manicotti* and *Ravioli.* Among the many seafood dishes are *Oysters Italian Style, Scampi* and *Broiled Trout.* Desserts feature homemade *Spumoni* and a delicious homemade *Rum Cake topped with a Delicate Cream Sauce.* The food is genuine Italian and its connoisseures fill the dining areas at lunch and dinner.

Increased popularity has necessitated expansion and a recently constructed larger La Riviera stands in support of the need to preserve Old World traditions.

Fettuccine Alla Goffredo

A LA - La Riviera

2	qts. salted water
1	lb. fettuccine noodles
½	cup melted butter
½	cup heavy cream
1	cup grated Parmesan cheese

1. Preheat oven to 450°.
2. Bring two quarts salted water to a boil and add fettuccine. Boil for five minutes.
3. Meanwhile put an oval serving dish in hot oven to heat thoroughly.
4. Drain the cooked fettuccine.
5. Add butter and cream to heated dish. Next add fettuccine.
6. Add cheese and mix with fork and spoon until all ingredients are well blended, making a very creamy sauce.
7. Serve immediately.

Serves: 6-8
Preparation: 15 minutes

A very good noodle dish!

Minestrone Genovese

A LA - La Riviera

3½ quarts water
2 t. salt *(or more according to taste)*
½ cup olive oil
1⅓ cups pinto beans *(frozen or cooked according to package directions)*
1 cup string beans (fresh)
2 stalks celery (diced)
1 carrot (sliced)
3 large zucchini (sliced)
3 large potatoes (peeled and diced)
1 bunch collard greens or ½ head cabbage (sliced)

3 large tomatoes or 1-15 oz. can plum tomatoes
1 cup romano cheese (grated)
¼ cup dried basil
2 cloves garlic
½ lb. macaroni (any kind)
   additional romano cheese (grated for garnish)

1. Bring water to boil; add salt, olive oil, beans and vegetables. Lower heat, simmer for thirty five minutes.
2. Meanwhile put tomatoes, cheese, basil and garlic in blender or processor to liquify. Pour mixture into soup and stir.
3. Remove one half of vegetables and put in blender or processor to liquify. Add to soup to make thicker. Continue cooking for additional thirty minutes.
4. Add macaroni, cook for eight - ten minutes.
5. Serve soup; sprinkle with more cheese.

— Continued —

Minestrone Genovese — Continued

Serves: 6-8 entrees
Cooking time: 1 hour 25 minutes (includes preparation)

A delicious version of traditional soup. Very hearty.

Saltimbocca Alla Romano
Veal with Ham

A LA - La Riviera

12   **small veal scallops**
12   **slices of thin Parma or Country Ham**
       sage (to taste)
4   **T. butter**
       salt and pepper
½   **cup parsley (finely minced)**
½   **cup dry white wine**

1. Pound the scallops very thin.
2. Place a slice of ham on each scallop and secure with a toothpick (do not roll up).
3. Sprinkle with sage.
4. Melt butter in a pan and brown the secured slices on both sides over medium high heat.
5. Salt and pepper lightly, remembering that ham is already salty. Sprinkle with parsley.
6. Place veal on a warm platter and keep warm.
7. Add wine to the pan and increase the heat. Deglaze* the pan, cooking rapidly for several minutes.
8. Spoon this liquid over veal and serve immediately.

Serves: 6
Preparation: 45 minutes (includes cooking)

A must for veal lovers!

* See Glossary of Terms

Scampi

A LA - La Riviera

2 lbs. large raw shrimp
½ cup butter
1 t. salt
6 cloves garlic
¼ cup fresh parsley (chopped)
3 T. lemon juice
1 T. paprika
6 lemon wedges

1. Preheat oven to 400°.
2. Remove shells from shrimp, leaving shell on tail only. Devein and wash under running water; drain on paper towels.
3. Meanwhile melt butter in baking dish in oven; add salt, garlic, one tablespoon parsley and mix well. Arrange shrimp in a single layer in the baking dish.
4. Bake uncovered for five minutes; turn shrimp; sprinkle with lemon juice and paprika and add remaining parsley. Return to oven and bake an additional 8-10 minutes. Do not overcook.
5. Arrange shrimp on heated serving platter and pour garlic butter from pan over shrimp. Garnish with lemon wedges.

Serves: 4-6
Preparation: 15 minutes
Baking: 15 minutes

Yummy shrimp dish!

Veal Piccata

A LA - La Riviera

12	**veal scallops** *(beaten thin and flat)*
¼	**cup flour**
½	**t. salt**
¼	**t. pepper**
6	**T. butter**
2	**T. parsley (finely chopped)**
2	**T. hot beef stock or broth**
	juice from 1 lemon

1. Dredge veal scallops in flour, salt and pepper.
2. Melt four tablespoons of butter in frying pan; add veal and fry quickly. Remove to heated dish and keep warm.
3. Add remaining butter and rest of ingredients to pan, all the while scraping and stirring residue from bottom of pan into sauce. Stir well until sauce is bubbly, pour over veal.
4. Serve immediately.

Serves: 6
Cooking: 15 minutes

Romanoff's has closed since the first printing of this book, but many of its former patrons recall how it preserved the sumptuous and aristocratic legacy of the Russian Romanoffs.

The proprietor, George Huber, who captivated diners, came from a background as interesting as was his restaurant. He was born in a region of Poland that is now part of Russia and raised by a Ukranian-White Russian governess. His knowledge of foods was inherited from a grandfather who was granted the title, "Baron" by a Hapsburg emperor. George is affectionately called "The Baron" today.

— Continued —

143

Although we can no longer visit the elegant restaurant in suburban Metairie, we can orchestrate the following classic European and Russian recipes to the mild strains of Rachmaninoff and Tchaikovsky.

Crepes Normande ma Facon

A LA Romanoff's

6   **crepes** *(see LeRuth's recipe "Crepes a la Ritz" p. 154)*
6   **large, firm red apples** *(peeled, cored, sliced about ⅜")*
3   **T. sweet butter (divided)**
1   **cup granulated sugar**
¼   **cup Calvados or Apple Jack Brandy**
       powdered sugar
       melted butter

1. Prepare crepes according to LeRuth's recipe or your own favorite recipe. Keep warm.
2. Saute apple slices in one and one half tablespoons of butter over high heat.
3. When about cooked (barely soft) add white sugar and one and one half tablespoons more butter and cook until apples caramelize on the bottom.
4. Flame* mixture with Apple Jack or Calvados (pour liquor over apples and light). Shake contents in pan until flame dies.
5. Fill warm crepes with about two tablespoons of apple mixture and fold over.
6. Brush with melted butter; sprinkle with powdered sugar.
7. Reheat if necessary.

Serves: 6
Preparation: 20 minutes (does not include crepe preparation).
Cooking: 20 minutes

Very sweet and delicious!

* See Glossary of Terms

Coulibiac de Saumon Gastronomique
Salmon in Pastry

A LA Romanoff's

4	T. butter
3	ribs celery (diced)
½	lb. fresh mushrooms (diced)
1	small onion (diced)
1	clove garlic (diced)
¼	cup flour
½	cup sour cream
3	egg yolks (lightly beaten)
	salt and pepper (to taste)
1	large sour pickle (diced)
2	hard boiled eggs (chopped)
1	T. parsley (chopped)
1	pinch cumin (optional)
1	lb. puff pastry dough*
1	large salmon filet (skinned and deboned)
3	egg whites (beaten until frothy)
	additional dough pieces for decorating (optional)

1. Melt butter in saucepan; add celery, mushrooms, onion and garlic. Saute until soft, approximately ten minutes.
2. Add flour; stir until smooth.
3. Remove from heat. Beat in sour cream and egg yolks.
4. Add salt, pepper, pickle, hard boiled eggs, parsley and cumin. Set aside to cool. Preheat oven to 400°.
5. Roll puff pastry into a rectangle, double the size of filet.
6. Spread puff pastry with half of the vegetable/egg mixture in center.
7. Top with fish filet and spread with remaining vegetable mixture.
8. Brush edges of dough with egg white. Wrap fish by folding sides over envelope fashion.

— Continued —

9. Place seam side down in a double pan (one pan set inside another).
10. Brush dough with more egg white and decorate with dough cut outs, if desired.
11. Bake for about twenty minutes. If it browns too quickly, cover with foil.

Serves: 4
Preparation: 45 minutes
Baking: 20 minutes

Comments: Fancy way of serving a delectable dish. Terrific flavor!

* Purchase puff pastry by Pepperidge Farms or similar brand, in frozen food section of grocery.

Spinach Flambe Czarina

A LA Romanoff's

½   cup raw bacon (cut into ¼" strips)
½   cup green onions (coarsely chopped)
1¼ cups white vinegar
2   t. granulated sugar
2½-3 t. grey poupon mustard
4   T. vodka
¾   lb. fresh spinach leaves
½   cup fresh mushrooms (sliced)
½   cup croutons
    pinch of salt
    freshly ground pepper (to taste)

1. In a ten inch frying pan, saute bacon until cooked halfway. Drain off grease and continue cooking until bacon becomes transparent and begins to crisp.
2. Add onions and cook until onions are soft, but not brown.
3. Pour in vinegar and sprinkle in sugar. Stir until well mixed.
4. Reduce liquid until you can see bottom of pan when fork is passed through mixture.
5. Add mustard and mix until blended.
6. Pour in vodka and ignite*. Allow to flame.
7. Put spinach and mushrooms in salad bowl. Pour in dressing and toss lightly.
8. Add croutons, salt and pepper and toss again. Serve immediately.

Serves: 4
Preparation: 20 minutes

* See Glossary of Terms

The dean of southern chefdom and a native New Orleaner –
Warren LeRuth developed his proficiencies in bakeries, pastry
shops, aboard molasses tankers, on oilrigs, feeding the military's
heaviest brass, conduction research for industrial "heavies" like
Procter & Gamble and testing flavors from Boston to Texas.

In 1966 LeRuth returned to his hometown and displayed his talents in an unpretentious, Victorian home located fifteen minutes from the Vieux Carre in neighboring Gretna. Since then
LeRuth's has won endless acclaim including Mobil Five Star
awards, Holiday magazine awards and recognitions as New
Orleans' finest restaurant.

Warren-the chef and sons, Laurence and Lee-the cooks, are
preparing creative New Orleans/French style cuisine. The restaurant's departure from rigid traditions dominate the menu.

— Continued —

149

Some say the best dish is served in a bowl - *"Potage LeRuth"* uses soup as the vehicle to bring out the best in oysters and artichokes. *Crabmeat St. Francis* and *Oysters Brazilia* win approvals among the formidable list of appetizers. *Avocat Tropique*, one of two distinctive salads, consists of avocado and hearts of palm, topped with a vinaigrette sauce. Entrees include *Truite a la Termereau* - a braised trout stuffed with giant shrimp and tossed with *Sauce Admiral. Filet de Boeuf a la LeRuth* skillfully casts filet mignon, artichoke hearts and bearnaise sauce in what has proved to be a successful production. Entrees include *French Bread*–homemade daily, *Sauteed Bananas* and *Dauphine Potatoes.* Desserts are diversified and spearheaded by the homemade sherbet and ice cream. The wine selection is as broad as the price range. Included are many quality wines at affordable prices.

A table at LeRuth's is one of the most sought after tickets in town. Advance reservations are a must at 636 Franklin Street, Gretna.

Avocado Oliva

A LA - Le Ruth's

2   large ripened avocados
1   14 oz. can baby artichoke hearts
½   cup olive oil
2   T. tarragon vinegar
½   t. salt
**   pinch white pepper**
¼   cup fresh parsley (chopped)

1. Cut avocados in half. Discard seed and place on salad plate.
2. Fill cavities with baby artichokes.
3. Mix well: olive oil, vinegar, salt and pepper. Spoon over artichoke hearts. Garnish with chopped parsley.

Serves: 4
Preparation: 10 minutes

A tempting salad, or first course for avocado lovers!

Okra Omelette

A LA - Le Ruth's

1½   lbs. small fresh okra (sliced)
½   cup salad oil
12   eggs (6 per omelette)
1   T. butter

1. Saute okra in hot oil to remove all moisture (approximately twenty minutes).
2. Divide in two: set aside and keep warm.
3. In ten inch skillet, melt half the butter until bubbly; add six beaten eggs and cook until halfway done.
4. Add one half okra; cook until firm and fold in half; slide onto serving platter and keep warm.
5. Cook remaining eggs and okra in like manner and serve.

Serves: 4-6
Preparation: 35 minutes

An unusual and enjoyable flavor combination.

Barbecue Shrimp

A LA - Le Ruth's

1	lb. Chiffon margarine	¼	cup Rex Crab Boil*
2	T. creole or Poupon		(optional)
	mustard	½	t. Tabasco sauce
1½	t. chili powder	1	t. liquid smoke
¼	t. basil	2	lbs. raw shrimp (heads
¼	t. thyme		on if possible), cleaned
2	t. coarse black pepper		and deveined
½	t. oregano		(Chef recommends all
1	t. garlic powder		spices and herbs be
1	T. onion powder		Spice Island)

1. Preheat oven to 375°.
2. In a small pan melt margarine and simmer all ingredients, with the exception of shrimp, for five minutes.
3. Place shrimp in an uncovered baking dish; cover with sauce and bake twenty minutes, stirring occasionally.
4. Serve immediately.

Serves: 4
Preparation:
Cooking/Baking: 10 minutes/20 minutes

Comments: Delicious and unusual flavor.

* Rex Crab Boil is a spice used for boiling shrimp and crab.

153

Lamb Rack Herbs de Provence Amandine

A LA - Le Ruth's

2   **racks of young lamb**
¼   **cup salad oil**
1   **t. salt**
¼   **t. black pepper**
2   **t. herbs de provence***
1   **stick butter**
2   **T. good white wine**
1   **cup sliced blanched almonds (toasted)**
2   **T. parsley (chopped for garnish)**

1. Preheat oven to 475°. Remove cover fat from lamb.
2. Brush racks with oil and season with salt, pepper and herbs.
3. Roast in oven for thirty minutes, bone side down. Lamb will be pink. Remove lamb and keep warm.
4. Skim off all excess fat. Place pan over medium heat. Melt butter; add wine and stir to scrape drippings that are on pan.
5. Place racks on serving platter and top with almonds. Pour sauce over racks and sprinkle with parsley.

Serves: 4-6
Preparation: 15 minutes
Baking: 30 minutes

* A mixture of rosemary, savory and marjoram–found in spice shops and gourmet food sections.

Pannee Pork Chops and Lyonnaise Potatoes

A LA - Le Ruth's

2   cups white onions (sliced)
½   cup vegetable oil (divided)
1   t. garlic salt
2   eggs (beaten)
6   thin pork chops
⅓   cup flour
½   cup fine bread crumbs
½   cup butter
3   cups new potatoes *(boiled, peeled & sliced)*
     salt (to taste)

1.   Cook onions slowly in one fourth cup oil, approximately thirty minutes until limp but not brown. Set aside.
2.   Meanwhile, mix garlic salt into eggs, dip chops in flour then eggs and coat with crumbs.
3.   Saute chops in remaining oil over medium heat until brown on both sides. Lower heat and cook slowly until done.
4.   Melt butter and gently saute potatoes until lightly brown.
5.   Combine cooked onions and potatoes and season with salt.
6.   Serve immediately with the porkchops.

Serves: 6
Preparation: 1 hour

A delicious country type entree.

A LA - Le Ruth's

— Crepes —

2	eggs
1	cup milk
¾	cup flour
½	t. salt
1	t. sugar
	oil

— Filling (optional)* —

4	lemons
1	cup water
1	cup sugar
4	egg yolks
4	T. flour
1	T. butter
4	egg whites
	powdered sugar (optional)
	fresh tart raspberry syrup**

— Crepes —

1. Place all ingredients in blender and blend for two minutes at medium speed.
2. Pour small amount of oil in six and one half inch crepe pan. When heated pour in two and one half tablespoons of batter. Tilt pan to coat evenly; when edges begin to brown turn crepe over. Repeat until all butter is used.
3. Keep warm until ready to use.

— Filling —

4. Scrape the rind from lemons and extract their juice. Put juice, rind, water and sugar in saucepan and bring to a boil.
5. In a separate bowl, blend together yolks and flour to make a smooth paste and add to boiling mixture.
6. After the mixture has returned to a rolling boil, remove from heat and stir in butter.
7. Beat egg whites until stiff and fold into mixture. Fill crepes and fold them.

— Continued —

8. Place together on serving platter; sprinkle lightly with powdered sugar and glaze under broiler. Serve immediately with tart syrup.

Yield: 8 crepes
Preparation: 45 minutes

Crepe batter freezes very well.

* Use your imagination with fruit fillings, etc. Be creative!
** Crabtree Publishing's Test Kitchen Alternative: Simply heat one pint of fresh or frozen unsugared raspberries on low until hot. Pour over crepes. No sugar is necessary.

Estelle's Pecan Pie

A LA - Le Ruth's

3	**eggs**
¾	**cup sugar**
1	**cup white Karo syrup**
¼	**cup butter (½ stick) melted**
1	**t. vanilla**
1	**cup pecans (slightly chopped)**
1	**9" pie shell (unbaked)**

1. Preheat oven to 350°.
2. Mix eggs, sugar and syrup. Add butter, vanilla and pecans.
3. Pour into pie shell and bake forty five to fifty minutes.
4. Cool and serve

Serves: 6
Baking: 45-50 minutes

Delicious!

"Tip: For maximum flavor always shell your own pecans. Practically all commercially packed pecans are washed before packaging." Warren LeRuth

the Versailles

Restaurant

If a man is to be judged by the recognitions he receives, then Gunter Preuss, owner of the Versailles, is a chef whose sauce pans must be weighed heavily. He has won the plaudits of the Chaine Des Rotisseurs – an international gourmet society founded more than seven hundred years ago, the Societe Culinaire Philanthropique and the Bordeaux Society. He is former chairman of the New Orleans Culinary Art Food Festival, past president of the local chapter of the American Culinary Federation and elected to the Academy of Chefs.

The above mentioned accolades are more meaningful when your menu selections arrive at the table. For the appetizer consider the *Escargots*. The Versailles presents them in a hollowed-out loaf of French bread which is soaked in a burgundy and garlic sauce and covered with sliced green onions. Soups include *Cream of Leek* and *Artichoke*. The *Bouillabaisse* would please the most discriminating francophile. The *Duck a la Flamande* is braised and served in a sauce of Port wine and sour cherries. There are a number of veal dishes, each distinct from the other. *Veal Financiere* serves tender veal sauteed with sweetbreads, mushrooms and olives. *Veal Moscovite* consists of veal cutlet topped with scrambled egg, caviar and smoked salmon. Other selections include *Grilled Game Hens, Fresh Trout Poached in Vermouth with Shrimp and Thyme, Rack of Lamb* and *Breasts of Chicken Sauteed in Butter and Calvados*.

— Continued —

159

The Versailles is plush and European in decor. Free valet parking precedes your entering an environment of ornate woodwork, comfortable chairs, statuary, chandeliers, paintings and crisp linen.

The Versailles, voted one of the ten best restaurants in New Orleans, is located in the Garden District at 2100 St. Charles.

Leek Soup
(Begin several hours before serving)

A LA Versailles

1	**lb. leeks**
1	**qt. chicken stock**
½	**cup onions**
¼	**cup butter**
¼	**cup flour**
1	**bay leaf**
1	**clove garlic**
	pinch of thyme
	salt (to taste)
	pepper (to taste)
1	**cup whipping cream**

1. Wash leeks; cut green tops off and set aside. Slice white part into one eighth inch thick slices.
2. Combine chicken stock with green tops and simmer for one and one half hours.
3. In large pan, saute white part of leeks and onions in butter until soft. Add flour; stir until smooth and cook for two minutes.
4. Strain green leek tops out of chicken stock, then pour stock into leek-onion mixture.
5. Add bay leaf, clove, thyme and simmer for one and one half hours.
6. Season with salt and pepper and stir in cream just before serving.

Serves: 6-8
Preparation: 3 hours

Delicious cream soup!

Lemon Souffle

Begin several hours in advance.

A LA Versailles __

— Simple Syrup —

1	lb. granulated sugar
1	cup water (heated)

7	egg yolks (from large eggs)
	juice and rind of 4 lemons
½	cup tequila
½	cup white wine
3	cups whipping cream (whipped)

— Simple Syrup —

1. Combine sugar and water in sauce pan and heat until sugar is dissolved. Remove from heat. Use this syrup in next step.

2. In top of double boiler, over simmering water, combine egg yolks, juice and rind of lemons, tequila, white wine and simple syrup.

3. Whip until mixture reaches a smooth, heavy consistency, approximately fifteen minutes.

4. Remove from heat and cool in refrigerator fifteen - twenty minutes.

5. Remove from refrigerator and fold in whipped cream.

6. Freeze until firm, approximately three to four hours.

Serves: 4-6
Preparation: 45 minutes
Freezing: 3-4 hours

Tart, tangy finish to a meal!

Veal Financiere ___

A LA Versailles ___

6	**pieces of sweetbreads ***
6	**veal scallops**
	salt and pepper
¼	**cup flour**
1	**egg (beaten with 2 T. water)**
¼	**cup clarified butter***
1	**shallot (diced)**
1	**green onion (top included, chopped)**
1	**T. parsley (chopped)**
4	**green olives (sliced)**
2	**cups brown sauce** (see recipe in Glossary or buy packaged variety)
2	**T. red wine**

1. Soak sweetbreads for one hour in cold water and remove membrane. Season veal and sweetbreads with salt and pepper; dredge with flour and dip in egg wash.
2. Heat clarified butter in skillet and saute veal and sweetbreads until golden brown. Remove to dish and keep warm.
3. Saute shallot and green onion in pan drippings. Add parsley, green olives, brown sauce and wine. Simmer fifteen minutes.
4. To serve, place veal on plate; top with sweetbread and ladle sauce over all.

Serves: 6
Preparation: 25 minutes
Soaking: 1 hour

A fantastic veal dish!

* See Glossary of Terms

Jackson Square

Much like the pearl, Visko's had modest beginnings but grew in size and popularity. From four tables tucked into an "A-frame," Visko's is now a sprawling seafood restaurant recognized in the local press, the "New York Times", "Signature" magazine, and "Mainliner."

The oyster, appropriately enough, is largely responsible for Visko's success. The Vuskovich family, using the harvests of their own fishing boats, opened a small seafood cafe. Patrons were attracted to seafood still dripping brine. A reputation for fresh raw oysters, fried oysters on warm French bread and fried shrimp was established. The menu later expanded to include calamari, crabmeat, fish, oyster soup, seafood salads, New York strip steak, cooked vegetables and desserts.

— Continued —

Recognizing America's growing interest in healthful foods that still contain their natural juices and flavor, Visko's now offers steam-cooked meals in "The Steamroom." A special menu includes, in addition to oysters, shrimp and crab - Alaskan king crab, lobster, flounder, game hens, stuffed mushrooms and artichokes.

Visko's is located twenty minutes from New Orleans in neighboring Gretna. Situated on a grassy knoll, the building's low profile, wood exterior and tasteful landscaping are reminiscent of southern Californian architecture. The interior utilizes natural woods from around the world, soft lighting, comfortable seating and an outdoor garden visible from much of the restaurant's interior.

Reasonably priced, Visko's is located at 516 Gretna Boulevard.

Oyster Soup Visko

A LA Visko's

24	oysters in own liquid
¼	lb. butter
½	cup green onion bottoms
½	cup green onion tops
2	cups oyster water
1½	cups milk
¼	cup dried parsley (chopped)

1. Wash oysters in their own liquid; strain and reserve liquid (should be two cups).
2. In sauce pan melt butter and saute onion bottoms until tender and transparent.
3. Add onion tops and cook until soft.
4. Pour in oyster liquid and bring to a low boil.
5. Add oysters and cook until sides begin to curl, about three minutes.
6. In separate sauce pan or double boiler, heat milk until almost boiling.
7. To serve, pour into each bowl three quarters part oyster broth, six oysters and one quarter part milk. Sprinkle with parsley and serve immediately.

Serves: 4
Preparation: 20-25 minutes

Oysters Meaux

A LA Visko's

24 oysters
    oil (to fry)
4 English muffins (split)
12 slices Canadian bacon
1 cup Meaux Sauce (See Visko's Meaux Sauce)
    paprika (garnish)
4 slices lime
4 sprigs parsley

1. Place oysters in a fry pan with hot oil and fry until deep brown.
2. Preheat oven to broil. Arrange muffins, split sides up, on a baking sheet. Broil one minute (do not brown). Remove; lower oven to 400°.
3. Place three slices of Canadian bacon across each whole muffin. Return to oven for approximately three to five minutes to warm.
4. Place six warm oysters on each ham muffin and top with four tablespoons Meaux Sauce.
5. Serve immediately garnished with paprika, lime slice and parsley.

Serves: 4
Preparation: 10 minutes (add 15 minutes for sauce)

Meaux Sauce

A LA Visko's

3   whole eggs
½   t. white pepper
⅛   t. red pepper
3   T. lemon juice
2   cups vegetable oil
3   T. Imported Pommery mustard*
       salt (to taste)

1. Place eggs, peppers and lemon juice in blender; blend on high speed, approximately twenty seconds.
2. Continue blending and pour in oil drop by drop until oil begins to emulsify. Pour remaining oil slowly in a steady stream.
3. Remove from blender jar; stir in Pommery mustard and salt.

Yield: 2½ cups
Preparation: 15 minutes

A mayonnaise type sauce that is very flavorful. Serve with seafoods and meats.

* Pommery mustard is found in most gourmet sections. You may substitute any grainy, mild mustard.

Seafood Salad

— Seafood Salad —

1	cup boiled shrimp (cooled)
1	cup cooked crabmeat (cooled)
1	cup steamed fish (cooled)
½	cup fresh tomato (diced)
⅛	cup green pepper (minced)
⅛	cup green onion (minced)

— Dressing —

¼	cup mayonnaise
¼	cup Thousand Island dressing
¼	cup olive oil

4	large leaves romaine or leaf lettuce
2	boiled eggs (cut in wedges for garnish)
8	wedges fresh tomatoes (garnish)
	dried parsley flakes (garnish)

— Salad —

1. Combine seafood, tomato, green pepper and onion in bowl.

— Continued —

— Dressing —

2. Combine dressing ingredients; add to seafood mix and stir until well blended.
3. Line four salad plates with lettuce. Arrange three scoops of salad on each plate. Garnish with two wedges each of egg and tomato on each plate. Sprinkle with parsley flakes. Serve.

Serves: 4
Preparation: 30 minutes

A very good seafood salad. I especially liked the dressing.

WINSTON'S

Winston's and the New Orleans Hilton evoke feelings which are uniformly uplifting. The hotel re-etches fuzzied textbook illustrations of such architectural feats as Thebes and the Gardens of Babylon. A sloping glass superstructure serves as a backdrop to a nine story atrium that houses a diversity of scenes, sounds and an expansiveness requiring a supple neck to view in its entirety.

Situated on the hotel's Lobby Level, Winston's provides further departure from the delta's heavy air, the Vieux Carre and jambalaya. On rush the white cliffs of Dover, Trafalgar Square and *Beef Wellington*. Butlers with aplomb and maids in starched ruffles replace waiters and waitresses. Sommeliers tred deep pile carpeting with bottled ambrosia from a well-stocked wine-room. A piano's clear notes drift up from below. Finely crafted furnishings, brocaded linen, flowered china and a staff with ramrod bearing accompany tables that float warm glows from sturdy white candles.

— Continued —

172

A verbal menu with varied choices stirs images of the freshest produce and meats. Such thoughts bear substance. An avocado laden with shrimp on a bed of tomato and bib lettuce, confirms little time lost between wine, brine and diner. *Lobster Bisque* with parsley garnish stirs fantasies of bottomless bowls. A salad with grapefruit, breadfruit and tomato, shows pride in preparation. A heat dome's withdrawal reveals *Rack of Lamb* with cauliflower, potato and tomato. Baptized with roux and sherry, the meat is a showcase of culinary expertise. *Cherries Jubilee* and finely brewed tea conclude sufficient atonement for past dietary indiscretions.

Chef Gerard Thabius began formal training in France in 1960. Distinguishing himself in a variety of posts including tenure as chef to Charles DeGaulle, Gerard's presidential skills are now available to the general citizenry.

═══════════════════════════════

A LA Winston's

— Mushroom Duxelle —

½	cup onion (chopped)	1	lb. mushrooms
2	T. butter		(finely chopped)
3	T. olive oil	¼	t. nutmeg (grated)

4	filets mignon	4	slices Pate de Foie Gras
	(8-10 oz. each)		(2 oz. each)**
	butter	1	cup Mushroom Duxelle
1	lb. puff pastry*		(recipe above)

— Madeira Sauce —

1	cup brown gravy	1	shallot (minced)
¼	cup dry Madeira Wine	½	T. dry mustard

— Mushroom Duxelle —

1. Extract as much moisture as possible from onions by squeezing in a cloth.
2. In a small skillet melt butter in oil and saute onion until golden brown; add the mushrooms and nutmeg.
3. Continue to saute on high heat until the mushroom moisture is absorbed.
4. Adjust seasoning with salt and pepper. Set aside. (This may be kept in a jar in refrigerator until use).

— Continued —

5. Preheat oven to 350°
6. Melt butter and saute meat in pan one minute on each side.
7. Roll out puff pastry thin. Cut into four seven inch squares.
8. Place one to two ounces of pate on each square of pastry.
9. Place meat on top of pate.
10. Top with two tablespoons of Mushroom Duxelle. Fold the pastry together like an envelope and seal.
11. Place seam side down and bake at 350° for twenty minutes.

— Madeira Sauce —

12. Meanwhile, reduce*** brown gravy to about three fourths its volume.
13. Add Madeira, shallots and dry mustard.
14. Keep hot, but do not boil. Place cooked Wellington on top of Madeira Sauce on plate and serve.

Serves: 4
Preparation: 1½ hours

An absolute delight for anyone!

* Purchase puff pastry by Pepperidge Farms in frozen food section of grocery.
** You may purchase this liver spread fresh at meat market or canned in gourmet section of your grocery.
*** See Glossary of Terms

Red Snapper "New Orleans"

A LA Winston's

4 **(8 oz.) filets red snapper**
½ **cup butter**
4 **oz. lump crabmeat**

— Mousseline Sauce —

1½ **cups hollandaise sauce (see recipe p. 3 or prepare from package)**
½ **cup whipped cream (unsweetened)**

1. Preheat broiler.
2. Saute filets in melted butter until done (five to seven minutes). Top each with one ounce crabmeat.
3. Carefully fold whipped cream into hollandaise and top each serving with sauce. Glaze under broiler for one minute or less. Watch carefully. Serve immediately.

Serves: 4
Preparation: 15 minutes

Veal Oscar

8	veal scallopine (thin)
2	T. flour (seasoned with salt and pepper)
2	T. butter
1	lb. lump crabmeat (warmed)
1	cup Bearnaise sauce (see following recipe or buy packaged variety)
16	green asparagus spears (garnish)

1. Pound scallopine into very thin pieces. Lightly dredge in seasoned flour.
2. In a medium size skillet, melt butter and brown scallopine over high heat (approximately one minute per side).
3. Place two ounces of crabmeat on top of each scallopine.
4. Cover with Bearnaise sauce and garnish with asparagus spears.
5. Lightly glaze under broiler until brown (approximately one minute).

Serves: 4 generously
Preparation: 30 minutes

Simply divine!!

Shrimp Queen Victoria

A LA Winston's

— Dressing —

½	cup butter	1	onion (finely chopped)
1	lb. pork (finely chopped)	½	cup white wine
5	slices white bread (crumbled)		

— Cream Sauce —

½	cup sour cream	½	lb. mushrooms (sliced)
1	lemon (juiced)	4	T. parsley (chopped)

2	lbs. shrimp (25-30 count to pound, cleaned and deveined)	1	cup white wine
		3	T. shallots (minced)
½	cup butter	1	t. garlic (minced)

— Dressing —
1. In a large skillet melt butter; cook pork, bread, onion and wine until done (about fifteen minutes). Keep warm.

— Cream Sauce —
2. Combine sour cream, lemon juice, mushrooms and parsley. Mix well and set aside.

3. In another skillet, saute shrimp in butter and wine. Add shallots and garlic. Cook about ten minutes. Preheat oven to 400°.
4. Combine shrimps with cream sauce.
5. Place warm dressing in a casserole; top with shrimps and sauce.
6. Bake in oven for five minutes. Serve immediately.

— Continued —

Serves: 4
Preparation: 35 minutes
Baking: 5 minutes

We really enjoyed this unusual combination.

Bearnaise Sauce
(For Advanced Cooks)

A LA Winston's

5	egg yolks (large)
3	T. lemon juice
	salt and pepper (to taste)
3	T. shallots (minced)
2	T. wine vinegar
1½	T. dried tarragon
1½	cups butter (melted)
¼	t. tabasco

1. Fill bottom of a double boiler with water and turn to medium low.
2. Combine egg yolks, lemon juice and salt and pepper in top of double boiler. Whip yolks until light and slightly thick. (Make sure the water does not boil. Turn down heat if necessary.)
3. In separate pan, simmer shallots, vinegar and tarragon for three minutes. Slowly add to yolk mixture.
4. Reduce heat to very low. Add melted butter very slowly (drop by drop) all the while beating the sauce, until it resembles the consistency of Hollandaise Sauce.
5. Finally, add the tabasco.

Yield: 2 cups
Preparation: 40 minutes

Comments: An excellent version of this classic sauce, but difficult to make, which is why we have tagged it for advanced cooks.

The Last Portion

Those eyes that dwell on the dilated pupils of Michelangelo's "David" or a parsley garnish often find a creative effort's final embellishment the most provocative. These few remaining pages discuss locations around New Orleans that lie in the shadows of larger advertising budgets, ornate facades and neon signs. Like forget-me-nots in a forest of poplar, these perennial attractions carve warm and sustaining impressions.

Few establishments provide more within modest surroundings than "Angelo Brocato's Italian Ice Cream and Confectionary Parlor." Angelo, Sr., brought his Sicilian recipes to New Orleans in 1905 and opened at 617 Ursuline in 1923. Today Angelo, Jr., and his son Arthur are continuing the family flair for authentic spumoni, cassata, Terracino and such seasonal favorites as strawberry, peach, orange, pineapple and lemon ices. The display counter showcases homemade cookies and pastries. The cannoli, catalani, teta, biscotti d'regina, cucidati and sarriardi can both test and toast a facile tongue. A framed visage of Angelo, Sr., looks on approvingly as his freezers and pastry racks are drained daily by locals, tourists, hotels and restaurants. For those who suffer impatience the parlor provides seating and immediate opportunity to savor the Brocato tradition.

The "Central Grocery Co." at 923 Decatur Street has seemingly stocked everything but snake oil since 1906. Barrels, bags and crates are the order of the floor and vie for space with sacks and bins. One can sniff tiger sauce, Hungarian paprika, arrowroot and marjoram. Touch dried stockfish, salted cod, bacala and fluted lasagna. See bags of polenta flour, chick-peas, walnuts and almonds, all offering up aged wooden scoops. Tables of Norwegian flatbread, Spanish candies and Italian cookies stand before refrigerated cases that contain cheeses, hams, salamis and sausages. Luncheon hour growls can be quelled

— Continued —

with a variety of sandwiches. A favorite combination is the popular muffuletta and a cold root beer. The antipasto has been made fresh daily since the store opened and is easily located on the counter in a large bowl with the ceiling strung pulley clasped to its lid. A smooth hitching post, ice house and the original horseless carriage are all that is lacking at this repository of times past.

If Brocato's and the Central Grocery Co. stand in defiance of artificial flavoring and little green stamps, the "Cafe Du Monde" offers a battlement from which to face this country's franchised hordes of rolling doughnuts. Standing a twenty-four hour vigil opposite Jackson Square, the "Cafe Du Monde" fortifies her defenders on fresh cafe au lait and warm beignets. A non-partisan atmosphere provides a haven for the glib and glum, larks and nightingales, weary shoppers and post-party revelers. Some find it a refuge from an interminable sun or malicious cloud. People peepers can observe sidewalk traffic while feeling a bit Continental seated on the cafe's breezeway.

Within a healthy doughnut roll or one skip of a smooth beignet from the Cafe Du Monde lies "Jackson Square." While unappreciative pigeons further decorate Andrew Jackson's uniform, youngsters and adults have little trouble finding a variety of interests on the Square. The many artists whose easels outnumber Jackson's medals, are either putting portraits or architectural compositions to canvas. Visitors either enjoy watching the artists develop their talents or choose to pose for that portrait to hang in the den. St Louis Cathedral and The Cabildo, two of the more prominent buildings in the Square, are opened for regularly scheduled tours. To reward a patient child, the Puppetorium offers continuous shows seven days a week. An adjacent ice cream shop is flavored to satisfy the tastes of

— Continued —

young and old. Finally, it's quite common to devour sweets to the streetside antics of a pantomimist, the varied sounds of wandering musicians or a solitary guitar.

Finally, no visit to New Orleans is baptized with the water of the bayou unless a pilgrimage is taken to the city's soul. The rites take place daily at 726 St. Peter—a building whose dowdy exterior includes windows that beg tin cups. This outer appearance belies the wealth within. "Preservation Hall's" ministers all share a god-given gift of rhythm. With the aid of strings, sticks and keys they produce jazz of the black bourbon variety. Vestments of white shirts and suspenders accompany grey beards and faces that seem sad-fixed but for that moment of music. Nightly the congregation shares cramped shoulders and elevated spirits. The sound seems at home near the mouth of the river. Instruments and voices, both worn of youth's lustre, bridge seasons of sun, bring into focus smoky images of laborers working in the fields, docks and shallows and lessen the burden of heavy delta air. It is proper that Preservation Hall be visited last. Superdomes and sazeracs seem inconsequential baubles affixed to a body whose alluring character and longevity is due to an ancestry of strong people from varied stock, nourished on a land too rich not to return rewards with the minimal effort.

Around the corner from Preservation Hall, on Bourbon, small boys, dark of color, tease the street on feet familiar with a soft shoe. Moving within the framework established by a nearby sax, trumpet and bass, their bright eyes watch for tourists' tokens of appreciation. A light rain begins to fall and the slick pavement reflects neonized colors and the distorted images of onlooking pedestrians unmindful of the weather. Vendors, policemen and dogs with a nose for talent also watch and listen to the heels and soles lay down their staccato rendition. This city

— Continued —

183

thrives on its past, but this is the present and a street that shows no dampened spirit on a night of rain holds promise for the future.

Michael Grady

Glossary of Terms

Al dente

Cooked to a state of flexibility and yet firm, not sticky, 5-10 minutes. Homemade noodles, 5 minutes. If on shelf for long period, 8-10 minutes.

Bordelaise Sauce

Prepare the same way you do **Brown Sauce** except in addition to the onion, saute also ½ carrot (sliced), a few slices of celery, a sprig of parsley and ½ bay leaf (crushed). Add 1 tablespoon of ketchup or tomato puree and if you desire, a dash of Worcestershire and dry red wine.

Brown Sauce

The following is a very simple recipe using ingredients you most likely have on hand:

Saute 1 tablespoon of diced onion in 2 tablespoons of butter. Add 2 tablespoons flour to make a roux. Stir in 1 cup of consomme or beef bouillon and salt and pepper to taste. Cook over low heat, stirring constantly, or cook in a double boiler. Strain. Yields 1 cup.

Butterfly

Slicing against or across the grain to make it more tender. Also, to open up a pocket for stuffing by cutting through the middle of the side of a filet and opening up two flaps which can later enclose stuffing.

Clarified, Clarify

To make clear by adding a clarifying agent or removing sediment. In the case of butter, simply melt it over low heat. In between the foam on top and the milk solids which will have settled to the bottom of your pan, you will have a clear liquid. This is your clarified butter. Skim the foam from the top and discard. Tilt pan to gather your clarified butter. The sediment at the bottom can be discarded or used in baking if you desire.

Creme Fraiche

To make this slightly soured cream, you add 1 tablespoon buttermilk to 1 cup heavy cream. Let sit in warm place overnight - or about 15-20 hours. In some cases you may substitute heavy cream.

— Continued —

185

Demi-Glace

A reduced Brown Sauce.

Deglaze

To moisten a roast pan or saute pan with wine, vinegar, stock or water in order to dissolve the carmelized drippings from roasted meats, etc., so that they might be used in the sauce. To do this, scrape up the bottom residue into the liquid with a wooden spatula while cooking over low heat.

Dressed

Stuffed.

Fish Stock

Add ½ cup each of sliced onion, carrot and celery to three cups cold water and ½ cup white wine. Bring to a boil and add 1 lb. of fish bones, head, tails, trimmings, etc. Cook for twenty minutes and strain. In some cases you may substitute chicken stock or bouillon.

Flamber or Flambe

This process adds flavor to dessert and meat dishes. Light match to warmed liqueur to make a flame and burn off the alcohol. It's easy to ignite if you tilt the pan and touch the flame to the edge.

Flour (Browned)

This is great for gravies and sauces as it enhances the flavor. Simply brown the amount of flour you need in a cast iron skillet or other heavy pan, stirring constantly. Be sure the flour does not get too brown. It should be golden brown in color. An alternate method is to brown it in a moderate oven for 20-30 minutes till golden, stirring occasionally.

Garlic (Pressed)

Use a garlic press to squeeze out the juice and pulverise the clove. Discard the hull. If you do not own a press, you may mash the garlic with the blade of a knife or with the back of a spoon against the side of the bowl you're using.

— Continued —

Ignite

See **Flamber**.

Julienne

To cut in long thin 1½ inch strips. Should be thinner than French fries.

Lump Crab Meat

Lump crab meat or back-fin meat is taken from the body of blue crabs. It is white in color. You may use just about any kind of crab for most of the recipes included in this book, while doing so, however, it's interesting to keep notes on the difference in color, taste and even the texture. Claw meat, for example, is harder to shell and is brownish in color but is very tasty.

Reduce

To reduce the quantity of a liquid by simmering. This makes a stock or sauce more flavorful because it's more concentrated and is thickened.

Roux

Equal parts of flour and butter cooked - used to thicken sauces and gravies. (Melt butter over low heat. Stir in flour and cook over low heat for 1-2 minutes, until mixture is thick and well blended).

Saute

To cook quickly in small amount of fat.

Seasonings

(Adjust or correct) To make sure seasonings (salt and pepper, etc.) are correct to the taste - your taste. Add more if necessary.

Shuck

(Noun) - A husk, shell or pod. A shell of an oyster or clam. (Verb) - To remove shell of oyster or clam. You can do this by prying shall hinge open with knife and then inserting knife all around edge - or - place shells in hot oven for 5 minutes and drop in ice bath. Drain. Shells will open.

— Continued —

187

Glossary of Terms — Continued

Sweetbreads

The pancreas of beef and veal. Use veal sweetbreads in all the recipes in this book. Make sure they are very fresh.

A

B

C

(More sauces on next page)

T

V - Z

Prints of
New Orleans

The lovely scenes in this book are available signed by the artist on ivory linen, 8 x 10" and are beautiful for framing and gifts (showers, anniversaries, special occasions, house warming parties, weddings, and friendship and thank-you gifts; may be given individually or in multiples). Hang a grouping in hallway, bathroom, den, living room, foyer, etc.

One packet of 10 scenes costs $15.00 (includes postage and handling). Make check payable to:

New Orleans Prints
Crabtree Publishing
P.O. Box 3451
Federal Way, WA 98003

NOTES

NOTES

NOTES

NOTES

Crabtree Publishing
P.O. Box 3451
Federal Way, WA 98003

Please send me _____ copies of **A La New Orleans** and/or _____ copies of **A La San Francisco** and/or _____ copies of **A La Aspen** at $9.95 ($8.95 plus postage). (Washington residents add sales tax at 5% plus local transportation tax.)

Enclosed is my check for $_____.

Name _____

Address _____

City _____ State _____ Zip _____

☐ This is a gift. Send directly to:

Name _____

Address _____

City _____ State _____ Zip _____

(Fill out back)

Crabtree Publishing
P.O. Box 3451
Federal Way, WA 98003

Please send me _____ copies of **A La New Orleans** and/or _____ copies of **A La San Francisco** and/or _____ copies of **A La Aspen** at $9.95 ($8.95 plus postage). (Washington residents add sales tax at 5% plus local transportation tax.)

Enclosed is my check for $_____.

Name _____

Address _____

City _____ State _____ Zip _____

☐ This is a gift. Send directly to:

Name _____

Address _____

City _____ State _____ Zip _____

(Fill out back)

Other books will soon be available. Check the titles that interest you or tell us what books you might like to see.

A La Los Angeles _____

A La San Diego - La Jolla _____

A La Santa Fe _____

A La New England _____

A La Majorca - Spain _____

A La _____

A La _____

We will keep you on our mailing list to let you know when new titles are available.

Other books will soon be available. Check the titles that interest you or tell us what books you might like to see.

A La Los Angeles _____

A La San Diego - La Jolla _____

A La Santa Fe _____

A La New England _____

A La Majorca - Spain _____

A La _____

A La _____

We will keep you on our mailing list to let you know when new titles are available.

Crabtree Publishing
P.O. Box 3451
Federal Way, WA 98003

Please send me _____ copies of **A La New Orleans** and/or _____ copies of **A La San Francisco** and/or _____ copies of **A La Aspen** at $9.95 ($8.95 plus postage). (Washington residents add sales tax at 5% plus local transportation tax.)

Enclosed is my check for $_____.

Name _____

Address _____

City _____ State _____ Zip _____

☐ This is a gift. Send directly to:

Name _____

Address _____

City _____ State _____ Zip _____

(Fill out back)

Crabtree Publishing
P.O. Box 3451
Federal Way, WA 98003

Please send me _____ copies of **A La New Orleans** and/or _____ copies of **A La San Francisco** and/or _____ copies of **A La Aspen** at $9.95 ($8.95 plus postage). (Washington residents add sales tax at 5% plus local transportation tax.)

Enclosed is my check for $_____.

Name _____

Address _____

City _____ State _____ Zip _____

☐ This is a gift. Send directly to:

Name _____

Address _____

City _____ State _____ Zip _____

(Fill out back)

Other books will soon be available. Check the titles that interest you or tell us what books you might like to see.

A La Los Angeles _____

A La San Diego - La Jolla _____

A La Santa Fe _____

A La New England _____

A La Majorca - Spain _____

A La _____

A La _____

We will keep you on our mailing list to let you know when new titles are available.

Other books will soon be available. Check the titles that interest you or tell us what books you might like to see.

A La Los Angeles _____

A La San Diego - La Jolla _____

A La Santa Fe _____

A La New England _____

A La Majorca - Spain _____

A La _____

A La _____

We will keep you on our mailing list to let you know when new titles are available.